the fast
800
easy

the fast 800

easy

Quick and simple recipes to make
your 800-calorie days even easier

DR CLARE BAILEY
and JUSTINE PATTISON

Foreword by DR MICHAEL MOSLEY

SIMON &
SCHUSTER

London · New York · Sydney · Toronto · New Delhi

A note on ingredients: some recipes have been adjusted to account for Australian local produce and availability

THE FAST 800 EASY
First published in Australia in 2021 by
Simon & Schuster (Australia) Pty Limited
Suite 19A, Level 1, Building C, 450 Miller Street, Cammeray, NSW 2062
First published in the United Kingdom in 2021 by Short Books, an imprint of
Octopus Publishing Group Ltd

10 9 8 7 6 5 4 3 2

Sydney New York London Toronto New Delhi
Visit our website at www.simonandschuster.com.au

 A catalogue record for this book is available from the National Library of Australia

ISBN: 9781760857578

Recipe consultant: Justine Pattison
Recipe testers: Claire Bignell, Karen Brooks, Jess Blain
Nutritional analysis: Fiona Hunter
Project editor: Jo Roberts-Miller
Design and art direction: Smith & Gilmour
Photography: Smith & Gilmour
Food styling: Phil Mundy
Cover design: Smith & Gilmour
Hand models: Emily Sandars & Lily Smith

Printed in China by 1010 Printing International Ltd

The information contained in this book is provided for general purposes only. It is not intended as and should not be relied upon as medical advice. The publisher and authors are not responsible for any specific health needs that may require medical supervision. If you have underlying health problems, or have any doubts about the advice contained in this book, you should contact a qualified medical, dietary or other appropriate professional.

Contents

Foreword by Michael Mosley

Welcome to *The Fast 800 Easy*, packed with simple, tasty and super-healthy recipes designed to help you lose weight, fast. You may already be familiar with some of our previous books. But if not, this is the latest in a our series centred on the Fast 800 diet, an approach which involves safe, rapid weight loss and is based on many years of scientific research (more on this in a moment).

Clare and I have been living and working together for a long time. We first met at medical school in 1980, fell in love, and got married a few years later. Clare went on to become a GP, with a real interest in weight loss, as well as in preventing and reversing diabetes through diet; I became a TV presenter and science writer, with a deep interest in weight loss and healthy living.

I began to focus on this area in 2012 when I discovered that I had type 2 diabetes. I wasn't particularly overweight, but I did have a bit too much fat stored around my middle (visceral fat, the kind that's linked to diseases, including type 2 diabetes).

I managed to lose nearly 9kg (20lb) in eight weeks and get my blood sugar levels back to normal by going on what I called a 5:2 diet, cutting right down on my calories for two days a week and eating normally on the other days. This also stopped me snoring the house down, which Clare was particularly grateful for.

I later met up with Roy Taylor, a professor of medicine and a world expert in diabetes from Newcastle University, who explained that by losing all that weight, I had drained the fat from my liver and pancreas and reversed my diabetes.

Roy's studies had shown that going on a diet of 800 calories a day for eight weeks led to sustained weight loss of around 10kg (22lb) and big improvements in health. In his trial, for simplicity and ease, the participants had consumed their daily calories in the form of meal replacement shakes, before returning to more normal eating.

Inspired by this, Clare began asking her overweight patients if they would like to try the 800-calorie approach, but with real food, based on a low-carb, Mediterranean-style diet (high in protein and fibre, and rich in nutrients). She gave them recipes to try and they were delighted to discover how filling her low-calorie meals were, and how tasty. They were especially pleased with how quickly they lost weight and saw improvements in their blood sugar levels, blood pressure and cholesterol.

And then a few years ago, Clare contacted Professor Susan Jebb, a world authority on weight loss from the University of Oxford. Professor Jebb had, like Professor Taylor, carried out a trial in overweight and obese patients using meal replacement shakes, and shown average weight loss, sustained at one year, of over 10kg (22lb).

But would it work as well if you did the diet with real food? Clare worked with Professor Jebb to set up the 'Diamond' study involving overweight patients with type 2 diabetes. Their low-carb approach meant eggs for breakfast rather than toast or cornflakes, and having a salad with fish or chicken for lunch instead of a sandwich.

When the Diamond study was published in April 2020 it showed that those sticking to a diet of 800–1000 calories a day for two months lost an average of 9.5kg (20lb), which was almost five times more weight than those following standard advice (the control group); and, unlike the control group, they also saw big improvements in blood sugar levels and blood pressure.

At the same time, Clare and I, with the help of doctors based in the UK and in Australia, created an online programme, which you can find at thefast800.com. This provides weekly menus (which you adjust to suit your personal preferences), an activity programme and professional support.

So far almost 20,000 people have completed the programme and, based on tracking their data, we have found that people tend to follow a fairly reliable pattern: losing a lot of weight to start off with, and then continuing to lose weight more steadily, as they switch from the rapid weight-loss phase over to what we call The Way of Life. So far, the data shows that, at the end of the 12-week programme, people have lost an average of 9.5kg (20lb), and there is evidence from people who sign up for the maintenance programme of further steady weight loss at nine months and beyond.

We love feedback, and we have received lots of it. People like Anne, who wrote in to say, 'One word – brilliant! I lost 28lb (12.7kg) in 9–10 weeks and 7 inches (17.8cm) off my waist. Also dropped 2 clothes sizes. Love this programme!'

Or Mike, a former headteacher, who lost 20kg (44lb) and 5 inches (13cm) from his waist, and who has now kept it off for more than three years. 'I have learnt so much about food and about which are good for me, personally. My life has been transformed.'

I do believe that the Fast 800 approach represents a new and highly effective way to help people lose weight and keep it off, fast and safely. I hope you enjoy these recipes as much as we do, and please do get in contact with us via the website or via Clare's Instagram account (@drclarebailey), where you can watch her, some of our kids and me cooking some of her delicious meals.

What is the *Fast 800 Easy*?

This book was conceived during the early months of the pandemic. Aware of the impact that being stuck inside, grazing on food and box sets, was having on people's waists and blood sugar levels, I realised it might be helpful to produce a super-simple new companion cookbook to the *Fast 800* to make it as easy as possible for people to eat healthily and lose weight, if they wanted to.

I've been a GP for more than 30 years, during which time I have seen a lot of change. Some good, some bad. One of the most striking changes has been a dramatic increase in the average patient's waist size, as well as a doubling in rates of type 2 diabetes. Although there is an element of personal responsibility in how we manage our health, I don't blame people for succumbing to temptation; I blame the junk food culture which pervades our world, a culture which encourages people to eat far too many sugary processed foods.

Most people are aware of the link between waist size and the risk of chronic diseases, like heart disease, cancer and diabetes, but it has taken the arrival of Covid 19 to inject a new sense of urgency. It is now known that if you are overweight or obese, and particularly if you also have a chronic disease like diabetes, then you are far more likely to end up in hospital if you get infected.

During lockdown, we suddenly found ourselves not only having to cook all our meals at home, but also – because of restricted access to fresh ingredients – relying more on food from our store cupboards and freezers. It got me thinking: what could make food prep easier on busy days than knowing that you can create healthy, tasty meals from the ingredients you've already got at your fingertips?

So back in April and May 2020, I threw myself into working out what moderately low-calorie, low-carb, Mediterranean-style meals I could produce for our household of five from our existing stores. I started posting what we had for lunch on Instagram (@drclarebailey), sharing recipes with ingredients likely to be at the back of everyone's cupboards. Within weeks the recipes were being followed in thousands of households by people who were wanting to stay well and lose their lockdown weight gain.

There are plenty of occasions, of course, when there is no substitute for cooking with fresh ingredients, particularly when they are in season, but I now believe that we can get too hung up on the idea of 'fresh'. Tinned, bottled and frozen foods are often not only cheaper but also just as tasty, and, contrary to popular misconceptions, highly nutritious. If vegetables are tinned or frozen soon after they come out of the ground, the vitamins and nutrients they contain are captured in optimum condition and 'locked in'; whereas fresh veg and fruit left sitting on the supermarket shelf or in our fridges degrade and break down quite fast.

Happily, many of the principle ingredients of a Mediterranean diet – oily fish, nuts, olive oil, beans, lentils and wholegrains – can be freezer or store-cupboard staples. Fish is delicious fresh, of course, but it can be bought far more cheaply frozen or tinned. And, if you like fermented foods, which we do, then these too can live very well for a long time in the fridge.

I also wanted to make life easier for those who are in households where not everyone is following the Fast 800. So many of the recipes can be added to, or bolstered with more carbs for family members who are not trying to lose weight. That way you can all sit down and eat together, and avoid cooking lots of different meals.

The Covid-19 virus has underlined how important a healthy diet is for all of us. What we eat matters, not just for our weight and metabolic health, but also for maintaining an effective immune system to fight off infections. To shore up our immunity, we need to support our gut microbiome, those trillions of bugs that live in the large intestine. Food can be a powerful medicine. Eat a highly processed sugary diet and you knock off the good health-promoting bugs in your microbiome. Eat a varied diet with plenty of vegetables and fibre and you will be feeding up the good guys.

To keep your microbiome healthy and happy, I have included foods that will help it thrive – lots of lovely vegetables, as well as moderate amounts of beans, pulses and wholegrains. The latter are particularly high in fibre. As complex carbohydrates, they may add a few extra calories and carbs, but it's worth it (and vital if you are vegetarian). So, I slip chickpeas into a chicken curry or toss them into a salad, and add lentils here and there. Most people find they get to love this way of eating and feel so much better for it.

This book is for all of you out there who are juggling busy lives and have limited time to cook; for less eager cooks, who want simplicity; or for others who, like me, don't have the patience to spend hours at the stove and prefer to cut corners and do less washing up but still want to eat healthily.

Many of the recipes derive from my posts on Instagram during lockdown when we started sharing our lunches. The kids, now young adults, helped a lot with this, and gave honest feedback. And it was thrilling to find my Instagram followers also sharing their versions.

I have been incredibly lucky to team up again with acclaimed food writer Justine Pattison for further inspiration and for rigorous testing of all the recipes, to ensure they taste great and are easy to prepare. This book – like the last one – has benefited hugely from her years of wisdom, expertise and good humour, for which I am enormously grateful.

I hope you enjoy this way of eating, whether you are starting your weight-loss journey, looking for new recipes or just interested in the low-carb, Med-style diet as a healthy way of life going forwards.

Clare x

A note from Justine Pattison

It has been a great pleasure to work with Clare again, on this book.

This time we have made everything even easier, by including many one pot dishes, as well as healthy and accessible staples that can be put together from the store cupboard and freezer. We've simplified classic dishes and made the most of ready-prepared ingredients to add flavour with very little effort. So, you can expect to see more ready-mixed pastes and sauces, such as harissa and pesto, as well as tinned foods, nuts and seeds. Ingredients that are easy to buy, last for ages and can be used in a variety of ways.

We've also added prep and cook times, so you have a rough idea of how long each recipe is likely to take. The prep time is the hands-on stuff, like peeling veg or weighing out ingredients, and the cook time encompasses anything on the hob or in the oven. Often, you can quickly knock something together and then leave it bubbling in the oven while you do other things.

These are the sort of recipes that will fit easily into everyday life, while also helping with weight loss. We very much hope they will become your go-to meals.

Making your 800-calorie days even easier

Although embarking on an 800-calorie diet can be a challenge at first, we have tried to make it as do-able as possible, offering filling recipes that are tasty and quick to cook.

The great thing about the Fast 800 programme is that it is highly flexible. It involves three phases: first, the rapid weight-loss phase, where you eat around 800–850cals a day for anything between 2 and 12 weeks; then the New 5:2, a less intensive, intermittent-fasting phase, where you eat 800 calories on just a few days a week; and, finally, the maintenance phase, where you continue with the tasty, healthy, Mediterranean-style way of eating, exercising portion control but not having to count calories.

How long you stay on any of these phases is up to you. It is a programme that you can tailor to your own needs and lifestyle. The rapid weight-loss phase, for example, will not suit everyone. Some prefer to skip this phase and go straight to the New 5:2. People also approach their fasting days in different ways. Some like to spread their 800 calories over three meals. Others find it easier to eat their calories over two, with a late morning brunch and an early evening meal. Likewise, some people prefer to consume up to half their calories as meal replacement shakes. Others want real food.

Whatever your chosen approach, there should be something here for everyone. The recipes are arranged according to meal types – breakfast, light bites, soups, main dishes (with meat, fish and meat-free options and sides) and even the occasional treat. Calorie counts have all been colour-coded to make it easy for you to put together your daily 800. Make use of the prep and cooking times – it really helps on your fasting days to be able to plan your eating in advance. That way, you are far less likely to succumb to temptation or end up snacking while you are cooking. And, to keep things as flexible as possible, there are lots of tips on how to adapt the food for non-fast days or when you are eating with friends or family (see page 242). Many of the recipes are also gluten-free and include some dairy-free and vegetarian swaps.

The Fast 800 is based on the best diet in the world

Unlike the sweet and highly processed diet adopted by the Western world over the last 50 years – which has been at great cost to our health – the Fast 800 is based on a lowish-carb, Mediterranean-style way of eating, which takes us closer to the unprocessed diets of our grandparents. Research has shown it to be one of the healthiest diets on the planet.

The Med-style diet is also one of the key reasons why the Fast 800 diet is so sustainable. Unlike a low-fat diet, with the Fast 800 you can enjoy plenty of olive oil, nuts, seeds and oily fish, as well as avocado, and some full-fat cheese or yoghurt – all the kinds of ingredients that make food tasty and filling.

While 'lowish' in carbohydrates, it is not a seriously restrictive diet, where you have to give up everything that contains carbs.

However, it does mean cutting right back on sugary foods, as well as starchy carbs, such as white bread, white pasta, rice, cereals and potatoes, since these readily convert to sugars in your body.

Fortunately, the Med-style way of eating is also a great way to support your gut microbiome because it includes plenty of fibre. That's why our recipes contain lots of tasty vegetables, some fruit, as well as some wholegrains, beans and lentils.

Incidentally, most cuisines can be adapted to the principles of the Med-style approach, whether it be Indian, Chinese or Nordic. In fact, the latter are now more likely to eat a moderately low-carb Mediterranean-style diet than the Italians themselves, who sadly have adopted a less healthy, more processed, Western diet, and their weight is soaring.

So, what's out and what's in?

For the past 50 years we have been told to keep our consumption of fat to a minimum for fear that it will block our arteries and cause a heart attack. To compensate for this, we were encouraged to eat at least a third of our calories as starchy carbohydrates.

Likewise, the official line has commonly been to eat three meals a day, with snacks between meals and before bed if we got hungry. As a result, many of us are eating six times a day, leaving our metabolism constantly battling to keep sugar levels in the normal range. And given that most of us eat more than we burn, these extra calories usually end up getting stored as fat.

However, the good news is that in the past decade there has been a whole body of exciting new research that has turned standard dietary advice on its head. Studies have shown that, unlike the widely advocated 'slow and steady' approach, rapid weight loss helps people lose weight faster, get closer to their goal and keep the weight off.

Combine 800 calories with the moderately low-carb, Mediterranean-style diet and you have a highly effective way to lose weight, restore blood sugars and re-set your metabolism.

What's out

1 Starchy and processed foods

It is increasingly clear that we should avoid sweet, starchy and highly processed foods altogether. This is because the latter will undo much of the health benefit you get from eating healthily. You can chomp on as much broccoli, salad and beans as you want, but if you then eat a load of chips or processed snacks, these unhealthy foods will kill off many of the helpful microbes living in your gut microbiome. Be kind to these vital microbes and they will take care of you...

We describe the Fast 800 as a lowish-carbohydrate diet. This is because not all carbs are equal. Refined and starchy carbs, such as white bread or white rice, are very rapidly broken down, causing a spike in blood sugars and encouraging fat storage and weight gain. But not all carbs are bad. In contrast, more complex carbs, like wholegrains, beans or lentils, are slower to break down as they contain more fibre. As a result, they release less sugar and do so more slowly, leaving you feeling full for longer, while the fibre in them makes its way down to the large intestine, where those helpful microbes convert it into important substances that help keep you well.

2 Sugar – including hidden sugars

Sadly, we are surrounded by hidden sugars – they are found in all sorts of foods, including savoury snacks and takeaways, and can be very hard to spot. Check the ingredients in any ready-made convenience food, and the word 'sugar' may not appear at the top of the list, or indeed appear at all, despite it being included in significant quantities. Sugar often appears under alternative names, such as maltose, dextrose, fructose, glucose, lactose – of which there are 50–60 variations, many of which you won't even recognise. Add all these together and sugar can turn out to be the main ingredient.

Fruit, while it contains lots of health-promoting phytonutrients and fibre, is also a source of sugar. It's far better to eat the whole fruit than to have it in the form of juice, as the juicing process removes the fibre and turns a healthy food, where the sugar is released slowly, into a sugar hit. Do include a portion or two of fruit a day, but try to make it a low-sugar variety, such as berries, rather than sweet tropical fruits.

Alcohol is another challenge – it behaves like sugar, breaking down rapidly and causing a sugar spike. A single glass of wine can contain between 200 and 300 calories and ends up stored in the liver as fat, causing inflammation. Spirits tend to contain slightly less sugar. But because alcohol disinhibits us, we are more likely to eat crisps or go for a takeaway when we've been drinking! So, for many reasons, we recommend moderation and to avoid alcohol on a fasting day.

3 Sweeteners

The trouble with sweeteners is that most of them damage the good microbes in your gut microbiome. Sweeteners are many times sweeter than sugar, which means that, regardless of their low-calorie content, they maintain your sweet tooth and can increase your sugar cravings. Luckily, whilst on the Fast 800 diet, you will find your tastes change and you can enjoy treats with far less sugar as your palate adapts.

We use dried and fresh fruit, such as dates, figs, bananas and apricots, as a natural sweetener in some recipes. Unlike sugar, which is empty calories, fruit adds fibre and a variety of important vitamins and nutrients.

If you really must have a little sweetener, particularly in the first week or two while you re-set your sweet tooth, then the best one to go for is probably Stevia.

And what's in

❶ Protein

It has become increasingly clear that protein is key to regulating your appetite and to your general health. Protein is required by every cell and organ in the body, including the immune system and brain. It maintains your muscle mass and metabolism, as well as helping you to feel full. However, your body is unable to store protein, and it isn't able to tell you what you are lacking, so if you aren't getting enough, you will feel hungry and are likely to go on eating until you have satisfied your body's protein needs – and you may end up putting on weight.

It's important to get enough on a daily basis: you should aim for 50g a day (slightly more than what has previously been recommended), and perhaps 10–20g on top of that, if you are older or very active. And it is particularly important when on an 800-calorie day to ensure you get the minimum requirement of protein if possible.

To help you do this, we have included the protein content in all our recipes, which are carefully calibrated to help give you adequate amounts. We also offer suggestions for how to add protein top-ups (see page 239), so that you can adapt salads or veg dishes according to your own taste. Getting enough protein can be challenging for vegetarians, and even more so for vegans, who might be advised to take protein supplements or use meal replacement shakes on 800-calorie days, or even to consider increasing their calories to over 1000.

Using good-quality, protein-rich, meal-replacement shakes (see thefast800.com for options) will also help on days when you have to rush out the door with an instant breakfast, or as an alternative to grabbing a sandwich and crisps for lunch.

❷ Non-starchy veg

We know that there are numerous benefits to eating more veg. This includes an impressive 16 per cent reduction in the risk of having a stroke for every added portion. When you are trying to lose weight or control your blood sugars, it is best to stick to *non-starchy* vegetables, i.e. those that are lower in carbs and hidden sugars, such as spinach, cabbage and broccoli. And we encourage you to enjoy generous portions of these. Ideally, fill half your plate with steamed greens, salad, or any of the other vegetables on the list at the back of the book (see page 240). They are so low in calories that they can be eaten freely, without counting.

It's fine to add a dressing or sauce to your veg, but do remember to include those added calories in your daily tally (see pages 60 and 240 for dressings and suggestions for how to add flavour without adding calories).

That said, adding a little olive oil to your non-starchy 'free' veg is actually beneficial, as it can improve the absorption of nutrients. This is particularly important when it comes to the absorption of the fat-soluble vitamins A, D, E and K. In the big scheme of things, a little drizzle of olive oil here and there is fine. The message is: don't worry about occasional extra calories, if it helps you eat more veg...

And since we also know that variety is key to us getting the nutrients we need, you might take this opportunity to push the boat out and try new veg. By eating different phytonutrients (the health-promoting substances produced by plants), you will contribute to your metabolic health and to reducing inflammation. That's why we are encouraged to 'eat a rainbow'. Embrace as many different coloured vegetables as you can – red salad leaves, purple broccoli or beetroot, yellow capsicums, dark eggplants, as well as plenty of greens...

③ Fruit

Although fruit is a great source of important nutrients and fibre, go easy on it. Sweet fruits like mangoes and pineapple can be irresistible but they tend to put your sugar levels up. It is striking to see how often people with type 2 diabetes have been told to eat lots of fruit as part of their 5-a-day, when in fact grazing through the day on sweet fruits causes their blood sugars to spike and blocks any chance of fat burning.

Try to choose low-sugar fruits, particularly berries or hard fruit that contain plenty of fibre, such as apples or pears – and make sure you eat the skin, too, as that's where most of the health-promoting nutrients are found.

Fruit is also best eaten either with a meal or straight after, rather than as a snack, when it's more likely to spike sugars and be stored as fat.

④ Fibre

Most of us don't get anywhere close to eating enough fibre – the average in the Western diet is about half of the required 30g a day. To get what your body requires, you need to eat seven or more portions of fruit and veg a day, as well as some wholegrains, beans and lentils.

On a fasting day it can be a challenge to get enough fibre, but you will find that you get to love your veg, and a suitable meal replacement shake can also provide a top-up.

⑤ Natural unprocessed fats, mainly plant-based

When it comes to choosing oils, the least processed the better. Try and go for cold-pressed or virgin oils, as they are unrefined and retain their natural nutrients – although they are more expensive, so buy what you can afford.

For frying at high temperatures, use a good-quality canola oil. Extra-virgin olive oil is good for gentle frying and ideal for salads. Coconut oil, a bit like butter, is fine in moderation. I like the flavour it can give to some stir-fries and curries, and it provides a slightly sweet and flavoured alternative for baking.

As part of a healthy, Mediterranean-style diet, there are plenty of other 'good' fats to be found in the likes of oily fish, such as mackerel and salmon, as well as nuts, all of which have been shown to lower your risk of stroke and heart disease.

⑥ Dairy

We include a fair amount of full-fat dairy in our recipes because the evidence suggests that in moderation this is beneficial – and does not, contrary to some reports, lead to diabetes. Fermented dairy is best and full-fat products are less processed. Full-fat Greek-style yoghurt, for example, doesn't usually contain the starchy thickeners and sugars or sweeteners that are added to enhance low-fat products. We love the creamy richness of it.

⑦ Meat in moderation

Many of us are trying to eat less meat in general these days, particularly red meat, both for health and environmental reasons. But meat is an excellent source of good-quality protein and, as we have seen above, getting adequate protein can be a challenge on fasting days. So we have included a number of meat-based recipes here, as well as some veg-based ones that also contain small quantities of processed meat, such as bacon or chorizo, both to boost protein and add extra flavour. Try to buy better-quality, grass-fed varieties, if you can.

The Fast 800 – a quick recap

Rapid weight loss

We recommend that you start with this intensive stage, if possible. By sticking to just over 800cals a day, every day, for at least two weeks, you will kickstart your weight loss and improve your metabolic health. Why 800? Because this is low enough to induce mild ketosis, which is associated with fat burning, but high enough to ensure you get the nutrients you need.

After two to three weeks, pause and reflect on how it is going. If you are losing weight and not struggling with the diet, then carry on. You can continue this approach until you reach your goal, or for up to 12 weeks.

For convenience, some people find it helpful during this stage to make up some of their meals as shakes. See page 30 for recipes, or visit thefast800.com, where you will find a range of ready-made meal replacement shakes with a Med-style formation and decent protein content to help fill the gap.

Intermittent fasting with the New 5:2

When you get close to your target weight, or if you are struggling on the rapid weight loss stage, you can swap to an intermittent fasting pattern – eating 800cals on just a couple of days a week. Your weight loss rate will be slower on this regime, but it has been shown to be highly sustainable, and one of the most effective ways to lose weight and keep it off. We now recommend that, instead of reducing your calories to only 500–600, as in the original 5:2 Fast Diet, you stick to 800cals on fasting days.

The maintenance programme

Once you've hit your goal, you can continue on the healthy Mediterranean way of eating, not calorie counting but exercising portion control. For this 'maintenance phase', you can go on using most of the recipes in this book; just double up portions, add extra protein (see page 239) and a few tablespoons of high-fibre, unrefined carbs, such as beans, lentils or wholegrains (see page 241), here and there and you are set for life.

You can enjoy the occasional treat, but try to maintain a diet low in sugar and moderately low in starchy carbs to help prevent sugars creeping up or weight piling back on. The message is: relax a bit, but not too much! If your weight increases or your new outfit starts to feel tight, you know what to do...

Adding in Time Restricted Eating

TRE is a form of fasting whereby you extend your overnight fast to restrict your eating window during the day. There is evidence that going 12 or even 14 hours overnight without food gives your body and metabolism a chance to recover and to focus on other functions, such as 'spring-cleaning' old and damaged cells and helping you switch from burning sugar to burning fat.

So how do you do this? Well, if you stop eating by 8pm and don't start again till 8am – that is a 12-hour overnight fast (i.e. 12:12). You can then build up to a 14-hour fast, which means eating all your day's food in a 10-hour window (14:10). Many people find that eating in a narrower window makes it easier to manage a fast day. Either way, it is a good habit for all of us to get into, as calories eaten within a few hours of bedtime are more likely to be stored as fat.

	STAGE 1	**STAGE 2**	**STAGE 3**
	Rapid weight loss	**The New 5:2**	**Maintenance**
how TO FAST	**800cals a day** (for up to 12 weeks)	**800cals 2 days a week** (intermittent fasting)	**No calorie counting, but portion control** (consider a weekly fast day – 6:1)
what TO EAT	**Lowish-carb Mediterranean-style diet** (or replace up to half your calories with meal-replacement shakes)		**Lowish-carb Med-style diet** (watching portion size)
when TO EAT	**Optional TRE 12:12 or 14:10** (Time Restricted Eating)		

Getting started

1 Write down what you want to achieve.
Think about why you want to lose weight.
What difference will it make? What changes
do you want to see? And how important is it
to you? What will success look and feel like?

Your personal goal may be to lose the
weight around your middle; or to bring
about a general improvement in your overall
health, energy and mood. Reminding yourself
about what motivates you will help keep
you on track.

2 Kitchen hygiene. This isn't about
how clean and tidy your kitchen is. It means
clearing away temptation, hiding (or even
getting rid of) all convenience foods, snacks,
biscuits, white bread or whatever your
weaknesses are.

3 Tell people you are doing the diet.
This helps you to hold yourself to account
and increases commitment and success.

> ### SAFETY: Exclusions and cautions
> This diet is not suitable for teenagers,
> or if you're breastfeeding, pregnant or
> undergoing fertility treatment. Do not
> follow the diet if you are underweight
> or have an eating disorder. Discuss with
> your GP if you are on medication or if
> you have a medical condition, including
> diabetes, low or high blood pressure,
> retinopathy, gallstones or epilepsy.
> Nor should you do this if you are frail,
> unwell or whilst doing endurance
> exercise. (For more detailed information
> see https://thefast800.com/faqs/)

Side effects

Dehydration. The most commonly reported
side effects are headaches, constipation,
feeling light headed and fatigued. These are
mainly due to not drinking enough added
water. (For more on how to stay hydrated see
page 22.) As for constipation, again, keeping
well hydrated helps keep things soft – and
make sure you are eating enough fibre-rich
food. We try to include plenty of fibre in the
recipes in the form of non-starchy vegetables
and some beans, lentils and wholegrains.

Low blood pressure. Within days of
embarking on a low-calorie diet like the
Fast 800, you may see a drop in your blood
pressure, which is a common benefit, but
if you are on medication, particularly for
blood pressure, or have a medical condition,
it is important that you speak to your
health professional before starting as
your medication may need reducing
(see below Exclusions and cautions).

Feeling rough at first. Flicking the
metabolic switch so that your body goes
from burning sugar to burning fat can leave
you feeling a bit off-colour for a few days,
whilst your body's metabolism adapts. This
is known as 'keto flu' and will pass within a
matter of days. In fact, patients often tell me
that they then feel better than they had done
prior to starting the diet, with more energy,
a sharper mind and fewer food cravings.
Despite being on 800 calories, they find
they are no longer hungry all the time. If
your symptoms are severe or last longer
than a week or so, it would be wise to discuss
this with your health professional before
continuing the diet. See thefast800.com
for more information.

8 WAYS TO HELP YOU REACH YOUR GOAL

1 Avoid snacking between meals or late-night grazing. The trouble with snacking is that it reduces fat burning. If you must snack on a fasting day, eat a small portion of non-starchy veg, such as some sliced cucumber, broccoli or celery. Alternatively, try a few nuts (one portion is the amount that will sit on the palm of your hand) or a sliver of cheese.

2 Plan ahead. Willpower is fickle. Sometimes you have it, sometimes you don't. So best to assume it doesn't exist. Instead, plan to make things easier for yourself by ensuring that you have healthy, delicious alternatives to help you resist temptation. Don't go shopping when you're hungry and put any likely temptations out of sight (I have to hide milk chocolate from Michael) or, even better, just don't have them in the house!

3 Enlist your friends and family to support you. Explain what you are doing and why; perhaps you are wanting to reduce your blood sugars, or just to lose the extra weight that has been creeping up on you for years. Whatever your motivation is, the more they understand what you are trying to achieve, the more they can support you. Be specific: 'Please don't offer me cake/another helping/ice cream…'

4 Add in TRE. This will enhance the effect of fasting on your weight loss and metabolic health (see page 16 for details).

5 Be more active. This is really important for your general health – switch the TV off, get up and go outside, walk more and try some strength-building exercises, as this increases your metabolic rate. A word of caution, though: while exercise is great for cardiovascular health, mood, strength and sleep, it is unfortunately a lousy way to lose weight. You need to run 36 miles to burn off a single pound of fat. So, go easy on the hard stuff at first, especially on fasting days – save that marathon training for a non-fast day, or when you are closer to your target weight or have finished the programme.

6 Get enough sleep. We are increasingly aware of the impact that poor and disrupted sleep has on our brain and mood, leaving us irritable, with even less willpower than usual, and far more inclined to crave sweet and starchy foods. On average, people tend to consume around 350 extra calories after a poor night's sleep. Sleep deprivation creates a vicious cycle of weight gain, snoring and exhaustion. (See Michael's recent book, *Fast Asleep*, for the full lowdown on why we sleep and how to get more of it.)

7 De-stress. Do this where you can, and try meditation. (*The Fast 800* book has some great advice on this; or go to thefast800.com)

8 And if you fall off the wagon… Please be assured that all is not lost. We all have bad days when we return to unhealthy food choices, including my lovely husband! Just start again the next day. The sooner you get back on track, the better. Be kind to yourself, it's just a blip.

FAQs

Does it matter if I eat 2 or 3 meals a day on a fast day? On the whole, it is probably easier to do 3 meals a day, but it's a matter of what works for you. We would advise, however, that you don't go down to one meal a day, particularly if it's soon before retiring to bed, as your body is more likely to treat it as a feast and store more fat. See the meal plans on pages 244–8 for 2 or 3 meals a day.

Can I do it with shakes, too?

Yes, absolutely. We take a pragmatic view of meal replacement shakes. Eating real food is best, but if you are dashing out in a hurry and grabbing toast and jam for breakfast, or snatching a processed starchy lunch on the hoof, good-quality shakes are definitely preferable. They give you the protein and nutrients you need, and leave you feeling full. Do choose carefully as many of those available are full of sugars and contain inadequate amounts of protein (see thefast800.com for suitable low-carb, Mediterranean-formula options).

Should I take multivitamins?

Our recipes are carefully balanced to include all the nutrients you need, but on a low-calorie diet it is not always easy to combine your meals for maximum nutritional variety, so we recommend taking a good-quality multivitamin on your 800-calorie days as a back up.

What can I snack on? We would encourage you to avoid snacking between meals as this will stop fat-burning and may put sugars up. But if you must, nibble a small handful of nuts (unsweetened as they become very moreish otherwise!) or a few berries, or munch on a handful of non-starchy veg, such as carrots, cauliflower florets or celery. Alternatively, try a hot or cold drink to help keep hunger at bay (see suggestions on pages 22–3).

Can I exercise on a Fast 800 day?

Doing more exercise helps us in lots of ways, including improving health and mood, but it's not a good way to lose weight. If you are already doing exercise and feel comfortable sticking with it on a fasting day, carry on with your current regime. But don't start a new, heavy programme or do endurance exercise on a fasting day.

For those of you who have not been regular exercisers, you will find that as you lose weight you will feel better and have more energy and can get more active. Remember, it's not all about the gym. A lot of people surprise themselves and find they enjoy simple outdoor activities like walking or cycling.

Walking with brief brisk bursts of 30–60 seconds can be a great way to start. And adding in some strengthening exercises will increase your muscle mass and improve your metabolism.

I have lost weight but recently hit a plateau. What can I do? It is common for weight loss to happen in bursts. Initial weight loss can be deceptive, as early on it also includes fluid loss. But if you stick to 800 calories you are likely to go on losing weight. When the weight loss seems to stall, some people find adding in shakes as part of their daily quota on a fasting day can help. It's also worth checking that you are still in the 800-calorie zone. However, we are all different and some people will find that their weight loss is slower.

Can I eat bread? When it comes to bread, it's about choosing carefully, as white bread and a slice of seeded wholemeal sourdough are like chalk and cheese. You can occasionally have a thin slice of wholegrain, seeded or sourdough bread on a non-fast day, but try to avoid it on a fasting day. When you are buying bread, try to make sure the fibre content is higher than 7g in 100g.

Will I feel hungry all the time? For the first few days you are likely to feel hungry, but most people find that this settles as their metabolism re-sets. My patients often tell me how surprised they are that, despite such a dramatic drop in their daily calorie intake, within a week or two, they are no longer hungry all the time.

Is it expensive? Our calculations of a random sample of fasting-day recipes show the food to be affordable and likely to be cheaper.

Should I tell my doctor/health professional that I am doing a low-calorie diet? It is always a good idea to keep your health professional informed about a major change to your diet, particularly if you have a medical condition and/or are on medication (see Exclusions and cautions on page 18). It may help to print out a letter advising them about the diet, so they can monitor and support you in the process. This can be found at thefast800.com/healthcare-professionals. Most health professionals will be aware of the 800-calorie approach and will be supportive.

Some useful tools and tricks

- **A tape-measure** for measuring your waist and neck, and a set of scales; you might also consider investing in a blood pressure monitor.

- **Keto stix** (a urine dipstick to measure if you are in nutritional ketosis – i.e. burning ketones from fat instead of burning sugar); these can be helpful at first or if you hit a plateau. Please note that ketosis reduces after a few weeks, but weight loss continues, although at a slower rate.

- **A diet journal** – studies have shown that keeping a food diary can be hugely helpful when you are trying to lose weight. Try our book *The Fast 800 Health Journal* to help monitor your progress and to keep yourself motivated.

- **Cooking equipment – minimal!** A stick blender, some digital kitchen scales, a set of measuring spoons, a small and medium saucepan, a flameproof casserole with well-fitting lid, a wide frying pan or wok, a metal baking tray, baking dish (optional), medium bowl, vegetable peeler, spiralizer (optional) and a good sharp knife.

Hydration

Good hydration with minimal calories

Most of us fail to drink enough fluid. But keeping well hydrated is especially important on a fasting day as you are taking in less liquid with food and losing fluid when you burn fat. As a result, it's easy to get dehydrated, leaving you feeling exhausted, feeble, light-headed or suffering headaches.

On a fasting day you should drink an extra 1–1.5 litres of calorie-free fluids, mainly as water (and more if you are very active or the weather is hot). Sipping fluids can also distract you from cravings and reduce hunger between meals.

Do avoid drinks with sweeteners, as they can upset the good bugs in your gut; they are also likely to maintain your sweet tooth, as they are so many times sweeter than sugar and can leave you feeling hungrier.

Here are some lovely ways to add flavour without significant calories – drinks that can be enjoyed any time, and will not interfere with fat burning.

Cold refreshing drinks

We like water and drink it straight from the tap or filtered, and keep a bottle of water in the fridge. If you are inclined to forget to increase your fluid intake, try keeping a jug or bottle in the kitchen or at work – one that needs to be finished by the end of the day. Or carry a bottle with you. If you are not a fan of plain water, here's how you can make it more enticing:

● Drink carbonated water for a bit of fizz.
● For added flavour, put in a few berries or some fresh herbs, like mint, rosemary or thyme.
● Or you might add a squeeze of fresh lemon or lime, and drop a twist into the bottle.
● A slice or two of cucumber or zucchini looks and tastes refreshing.
● For a stronger brew, keep a bottle of cooled fruit or herbal tea in the fridge.

Hot comforting drinks

Try to avoid putting milk in your tea or coffee between meals, as this adds calories and interferes with fat-burning – although, straight after a meal, a dash of milk in your drink is OK. Between meals try taking your tea with a squeeze of lemon or drink black coffee.

For variety, try sipping fruit teas. Or make your own herbal infusions, adding a handful of fresh herbs, such as mint, thyme or sage, to boiled water.

I'm a big fan of **mint tea**, with its smooth feel and sweet scent. Mint grows wild in the garden or you can keep it in a pot and harvest the larger leaves. Steep some leaves in hot water for 5 minutes. A generous handful of mint leaves contains a surprising amount of nutrients, including iron, vitamin and antioxidants, which may help protect your cells from damage. Peppermint is also thought to improve digestion.

Green tea, meanwhile, has been shown to be one of the healthiest drinks on the planet. Thanks mainly to its antioxidant properties, it is thought to reduce the risk of heart disease, improve brain function, protect against some cancers, as well as support weight loss.

However, green tea is an acquired taste, as it can be slightly bitter (that is part of what makes it so beneficial). We like to drink green tea with some finely sliced fresh root ginger (1cm unpeeled) and ½ teaspoon ground cinnamon stirred in to add a delicate sweetness. Allow the tea leaves and ginger to steep for 3–5 minutes, then remove them before you drink.

Tips for using this book

● **Calorie counts:** These refer to one individual serving, unless stated otherwise. That said, please be aware that we include calorie counts as a rough guide only. There are significant variations between different nutritionists, counters and apps, so don't be too concerned by a few extra calories here or there.

● **To increase non-starchy veg eating and reduce calorie counting,** we encourage you to enjoy these low-calorie foods without counting calories. Pile half your plate with 'free' vegetables, such as leafy greens, salad leaves or celery, which have minimal calories but huge nutritional benefits (see page 240 for non-starchy greens and veg). Unless, of course, you want to add a dressing or a teaspoonful of extra-virgin olive oil – in which case, see page 240 for calories.

● **Suggestions for non-fast days:** We offer plenty of tips if you are on the New 5:2 or have moved on to a maintenance stage to adapt the recipes to make them more substantial (see page 244). These might involve simply increasing or doubling the portion size, or adding a few tablespoons of brown rice or lentils, an extra glug of olive oil, a slice of seeded bread or extra vegetables.

● **Make the recipes suit you:** These recipes are based on a Mediterranean way of eating, but can be adapted to fit different cuisines and tastes. Feel free to adjust them by using alternative flavours, or adding different herbs and spices – all of which have minimal impact on calories. The tastier and more satisfying your food, the more likely you are to stick to this way of eating.

Breakfast and Brunch

It's great to start the day with a protein-rich breakfast, even if you are extending your overnight fast and eating late morning or having brunch. If you prefer to skip breakfast, that's fine, too, but make sure you have plenty of fluid to keep well hydrated.

Eggs feature often in our recipes because they are low-cal and highly nutritious. But we also include nutty variations on porridge and granola, as well as omega-3-boosting fish and an almost full English... And don't forget the filling breakfast shakes.

PER SERVING | **176cals** | PROTEIN **4.5g** | CARBS **18g** | FAT **9g** | FIBRE **2g**

Fruit 'n' nut granola

SERVES **8** | **PREP** **10** mins | **COOK** **35** mins

30g coconut oil
1 tsp ground cinnamon
150g jumbo porridge oats
50g plain mixed nuts,
   roughly chopped
25g mixed seeds
2 dried figs (around 35g),
   roughly chopped
25g dried cranberries

COOK'S TIP

You can also serve the granola with around 75ml full-fat milk per 45g portion for 252cals. Adjust calories if using non-dairy milk.

This fruity, crunchy granola will power you well into the day. It's perfect served with yoghurt and berries. Top your 35g serving of granola with full-fat live Greek yoghurt (75g/100cals) and a handful of mixed berries (30g/11cals) for a breakfast bowl of 287cals.

1. Preheat the oven to 180°C/fan 160°C/Gas 4.

2. Melt the coconut oil in a large saucepan over a gentle heat, add the cinnamon and stir.

3. Remove from the heat and stir in the oats until thoroughly mixed. Scatter evenly over a large baking tray and bake for 15 minutes.

4. Remove the tray from the oven and add the nuts and seeds. Return to the oven for a further 10 minutes, or until lightly toasted.

5. Remove from the oven and leave to cool and crisp up on the tray. Stir in the figs and cranberries and store in an airtight jar for up to 2 weeks.

Nutty seedy porridge

SERVES	PREP	COOK
6	**10** mins	**6** mins

100g plain mixed nuts,
   roughly chopped
100g rolled jumbo oats
50g mixed seeds
50g mixed dried fruit
100ml full-fat milk, to serve

COOK'S TIP

For a creamier porridge,
add 1 teaspoon chia seeds
to each serving as you add
it to the pan. Add an extra
2 tablespoons water and
cook as directed. With the
additional chia, each serving
will contain 324cals and
12g protein.

A high-protein, fruity porridge. The rolled jumbo
oats are minimally processed, giving you slow-release
energy, while the nuts and seeds provide the protein
and fibre you need to feel full for longer.

1. Tip the nuts, oats, seeds and dried fruit into a large bowl.
Mix well together then transfer to a jar or other lidded
air-tight container.

2. For one serving of porridge, take 50g of the mix and place
in a non-stick saucepan. Add the milk and 100ml water,
place over a medium heat and simmer for 5–6 minutes,
stirring, until thick and creamy. Alternatively, put the
porridge, water and milk in a large microwaveable bowl
and cook on HIGH for 3 minutes. Stir and cook for a
further 30–60 seconds, or until thick and creamy.

3. Spoon into a bowl (if cooking in a pan) and leave
to stand for 2–3 minutes to allow to thicken.

easy ways
with shakes

Shakes are a super-easy and tasty addition to your fast day. They can help you get out of the door in a hurry knowing you will feel full, with the nutrients you need. They are also a great way to increase your daily protein. And when you don't have time to make them yourself, go to thefast800.com for ready-made meal-replacement shakes and soups. Here we offer a couple of basic recipes, with a choice of fruit and protein additions so you can design your shake yourself. The fruit shake is higher in sugar than the green shake, so probably best to enjoy in moderation.

Fruit shake

SERVES 1
2 tbsp full-fat live Greek yoghurt or
   dairy-free yoghurt (40cals/1.6g protein)
100ml full-fat milk or dairy-free milk
   (63cals/3.3g protein)
½ medium banana, peeled and roughly
   chopped, around 50g prepared weight
   (43cals/0.6g protein)
1 tbsp jumbo porridge oats, around 7g
   (28cals/0.8g protein)

Add 1 fruit:
50g strawberries, hulled and halved
   (19cals/0.3g protein)
50g raspberries (16cals/0.7g protein)
50g cubed mango (33cals/0.3g protein)
60g frozen pineapple (27cals/0.2g protein)
50g frozen mixed berries, such as strawberries
   and blueberries (20cals/0.4g protein)

Add 1 protein source:
1 tbsp ground almonds (44cals/1.8g protein)
1 tbsp chopped mixed nuts
   (60cals/2.7g protein)
1 tbsp mixed seeds (61cals/2.7g protein)
1 tbsp whey powder (25cals/5.5g protein)
1 tbsp chia seeds (71cals/1.9g protein)

Add any 1 optional extra:
1 tsp vanilla extract
½ tsp ground cinnamon
1 tsp finely grated fresh root ginger
finely grated zest ¼ lemon or lime
squeeze lemon or lime juice

1. Put all the ingredients for the basic fruit shake in a blender.

2. Add one fruit and one protein source.

3. Add an optional extra, if you like.

4. Add 3–4 tablespoons water or 3–4 ice cubes and blitz until smooth. Add more water, if needed, to reach your preferred consistency.

5. Serve immediately.

Green shake

SERVES 1
½ avocado, peeled, stoned and quartered
   (160cals/1.6g protein)
200g cucumber, trimmed and cubed

Add ❶ green vegetable:
25g young spinach leaves
25g young kale leaves, tough stalks removed
25g rocket leaves
25g watercress

Add ❶ protein source:
1 tbsp ground almonds (44cals/1.8g protein)
1 tbsp chopped mixed nuts
   (60cals/2.7g protein)
1 tbsp mixed seeds (61cals/2.7g protein)
1 tbsp whey powder (25cals/5.5g protein)
1 tbsp chia seeds (71cals/1.9g protein)
2 tbsp full-fat live Greek yoghurt
   (40cals/1g protein)

Add any ❶ or ❷ optional extras:
small handful fresh mint leaves
small handful fresh basil leaves
1 tsp finely grated fresh root ginger
finely grated zest ¼ lemon
squeeze lemon juice
good pinch crushed dried chilli flakes
splash Worcestershire sauce
splash Tabasco or sriracha sauce

1. Put both ingredients for the basic green shake in a blender.

2. Add one green vegetable and one protein source.

3. Add an optional extra or two, if you like.

4. Pour in 150ml cold water and season with a little salt and lots of ground black pepper.

5. Blitz until smooth. Add more water, if needed, to reach your preferred consistency.

6. Serve immediately.

PER MUFFIN | **71cals** | PROTEIN **5g** | CARBS **3g** | FAT **4g** | FIBRE **1.5g**

Cheese and spinach mini muffins

MAKES **12** | **PREP** **10** mins | **COOK** **25** mins

1 tsp canola oil, for greasing
1 × 400g can butterbeans, drained
3 large eggs
4 spring onions, trimmed and sliced
50g young spinach leaves
75g mature Cheddar, coarsely grated

COOK'S TIP

These muffins will keep well in the fridge for a couple of days if placed in a lidded container. They taste great cold, but can be reheated in a microwave or hot oven too.

A protein-rich savoury breakfast or snack that's easy to transport and can be eaten warm or cold. You could also serve the muffins with a mixed salad for a light lunch.

1. Preheat the oven to 200°C/fan 180°C/Gas 6 and grease a good-quality, non-stick 12-hole fairy cake/mince pie tin.

2. Place the beans and eggs in a food processor with a little salt and lots of ground black pepper and blitz until almost smooth.

3. Add the spring onions, spinach and cheese and blitz briefly on the pulse setting 3–4 times, or until just combined. You may need to remove the lid and push the mixture down with a spatula once or twice.

4. Spoon the mixture evenly into the tin and bake for 20–25 minutes, or until pale golden brown and firm to the touch.

5. Serve warm or remove from the tin and transfer to a wire rack to cool.

Scrambled egg stuffed mushrooms

SERVES | **PREP** | **COOK**
2 | **10** mins | **10** mins

1 tsp olive oil, for greasing
10 cherry tomatoes
    (around 100g), halved
4 large Portobello or
    flat mushrooms
    (each around 75g)
15g butter
4 medium eggs, beaten
small handful freshly
    chopped parsley or chives,
    to serve (optional)

A satiating, low-carb breakfast of creamy-tasting scrambled eggs on top of baked mushrooms and cherry tomatoes. Mushrooms are a great source of vitamin D, which most of us are lacking. It's easy to halve the quantities for one or double them up for a family brunch.

1. Preheat the oven to 200°C/fan 180°C/Gas 6 and line a baking tray with foil, then drizzle with a little oil.

2. Place the tomatoes and mushrooms on the tray, cut side up, and bake for 10 minutes, or until softened.

3. Meanwhile, melt the butter in a small, non-stick saucepan over a low heat. Tip the eggs into the saucepan and season with salt and ground black pepper. Cook for about 2 minutes, stirring regularly, until lightly set.

4. Remove the tray from the oven. Divide the mushrooms between two plates, tipping away any liquid that may have risen to the surface. Add the tomatoes, top with the eggs and sprinkle with the herbs, if using, to serve.

easy ways
with eggs

When you are fasting, it is important to include a good portion of protein in your meal and one of the best ways to do this is to include eggs in your diet – they are low-carb, high-protein and incredibly nutritious. If your eggs aren't fridge-cold, you will need to reduce the cooking time slightly. Whether you are scrambling, poaching, boiling or making an omelette, try these easy combinations for a more varied and delicious breakfast.

Egg breakfast

SERVES 1
2 large eggs (184cals/17.6g protein)

Add large handful non-starchy veg:
75g long-stemmed broccoli or broccoli florets
75g asparagus
75g green beans, trimmed
75g zucchini
2 Portobello mushrooms
75g small chestnut (or button) mushrooms
50g roasted capsicums
20g young spinach leaves

Extra protein:
50g smoked salmon (92cals/11.5g protein)
50g cooked and peeled cold-water prawns
**   (35cals/7.7g protein)**
1 rasher smoked back bacon (61cals/5g protein)
1 tbsp grated Cheddar, around 10g
**   (41cals/2.5g protein)**

Add any ❶ or ❷ optional extras:
small handful fresh chives
small handful fresh parsley
small handful fresh coriander
½ tsp mustard seeds
½ tsp ground turmeric
½ tsp ground cumin
½ tsp ground coriander
good pinch crushed dried chilli flakes

Poach

1. Third fill a saucepan with water and bring to a gentle simmer.

2. Break the eggs gently into the pan one at a time. Cook over a very low heat, with the water hardly bubbling, for 3–4 minutes, or until the whites are set and the yolks remain runny.

3. Meanwhile, prepare your non-starchy veg to serve alongside. You could place a non-stick pan over a medium heat and fry mushrooms or griddle thick slices of zucchini for 3 minutes, turning halfway through. You could also steam your choice of green veg.

4. Drain the eggs with a slotted spoon and place alongside the veg. Season well with a pinch of salt and ground black pepper. Serve with some extra protein and fresh herbs, if you like.

Scramble

1. Beat the eggs in a small bowl.

2. Melt a teaspoon of butter (34cals) or heat a teaspoon of olive oil (27cals) in a small, non-stick saucepan over a low heat. Tip the eggs into the saucepan and season with salt and ground black pepper. Add a spice, if you like. Cook for about 2 minutes, stirring regularly, until lightly set.

3. At this point, you can add some non-starchy veg and/or protein to your scamble. Try stirring fresh spinach or smoked salmon through the eggs before serving, or use slices of griddled zucchini instead of toast and top with the seasoned egg.

Or make an omelette

1. Whisk the eggs in a small bowl and season well with ground black pepper and a pinch of salt, and any spice or fresh herbs, if using.

2. Melt a teaspoon of butter (34cals) or heat a teaspoon oil (27cals) in a small non-stick frying pan.

3. Pour the eggs into the pan and leave to cook for a few seconds. Using a wooden spoon, draw the egg in from the sides of the pan towards the centre and let the uncooked egg run to fill its place. Cook for 2 minutes until almost set.

4. Now add your choice of non-starchy veg and/or protein. Try scattering prawns, strips of roasted capsicum or a large handful fresh spinach on top of the omelette. Cook to heat through for 1–2 minutes more.

5. Fold the omelette in the pan, then serve.

PER SERVING	**300cals**	PROTEIN **23g**	CARBS **2.5g**	FAT **21.5g**	FIBRE **1.5g**

Jalapeño, spinach and Parmesan omelette

SERVES	PREP	COOK
2	**10** mins	**8** mins

1 tbsp olive oil

½ medium onion, peeled and finely sliced

2 heaped tbsp sliced red or green jalapeño peppers from a jar (around 30g), drained and roughly chopped

2 balls frozen leaf spinach (around 115g), thawed and drained, or a large handful fresh young spinach leaves

4 large eggs

20g Parmesan, finely grated

COOK'S TIP

You will need a pan with a diameter of around 20cm. If you only have a larger frying pan, double the ingredients and save half the omelette for the following day. Reheat gently in the microwave or serve cold.

This is one of our favourite recipes. The jalapeño peppers really make the omelette sing. Enjoy it as a flavourful, mouth-watering breakfast. Or have it for lunch with half a plateful of green and coloured salad.

1. Heat the oil in a non-stick frying pan, add the onion and gently fry over a low-medium heat for 2–3 minutes, or until softened, stirring occasionally. Stir in the jalapeño peppers and spinach and cook for a further 1–2 minutes, until heated through.

2. Meanwhile, whisk the eggs in a small bowl and season with ground black pepper. Pour into the pan leave to cook for a few seconds.

3. Using a wooden spoon, draw the egg in from the sides of the pan towards the centre and let the uncooked egg run to fill its place. Cook for 2 minutes until almost set, then sprinkle with the Parmesan and cook for a further 1–2 minutes, or until melted.

4. Fold the omelette in the pan, then cut in half and divide between two plates.

Smoked haddock brunch pots

SERVES **2** | **PREP** **10** mins | **COOK** **20** mins

½ tsp butter or a little olive oil,
   for greasing
100g young spinach leaves
125g smoked haddock fillet
   (undyed), skinned and cut
   into roughly 1.5cm chunks
2 spring onions, trimmed
   and finely sliced
4 tbsp full-fat crème fraîche
   (around 50g)
2 medium eggs

COOK'S TIP

You can use 2 balls frozen
leaf spinach for this recipe
instead of fresh. Thaw
and drain thoroughly
before using.

These brunch pots make a wonderfully indulgent start
to the day. On a non-fast day, serve them with a thin
slice of wholegrain bread.

1. Preheat the oven to 200°C/fan 180°C/Gas 6 and lightly
grease two deep ramekins or individual pie dishes – big
enough to hold 250ml water. Place on a baking tray.

2. Place the spinach in a colander in the sink and pour
just-boiled water over the top until it softens. Otherwise,
you can soften it in the microwave. Leave to stand until
cool enough to handle, squeeze the leaves to remove as
much water as possible.

3. Place the spinach in a medium mixing bowl. Add the
haddock, onions and crème fraîche, season with ground
black pepper and toss together lightly. (There's no need
for salt as the fish is salty enough.)

4. Divide between the two ramekins and make a dip in
the centre with the back of a spoon. Crack an egg into
each dip, season again with black pepper and cover the
dishes tightly with greased foil. Bake for 20 minutes,
or until the eggs are just set.

5. Leave to stand for a few minutes before serving.

| PER SERVING | **250cals** | PROTEIN **12.5g** | CARBS **1g** | FAT **21g** | FIBRE **3g**

Poached egg with avocado and bacon

SERVES **2** | PREP **10** mins | COOK **6** mins

2 medium eggs, fridge-cold
2 rashers streaky bacon,
   halved
1 small avocado, peeled,
   stoned and sliced
½–1 tsp lemon or lime juice
pinch crushed dried chilli
   flakes (optional)

COOK'S TIP

If you aren't using fridge-cold eggs, reduce the cooking time slightly. It is important to use very fresh eggs or the whites may disintegrate when you poach them and be less attractive to eat.

A surprisingly satisfying breakfast. If you are eating this on a non-fast day, sprinkle 1 tablespoon toasted mixed seeds over the egg before serving.

1. Third fill a medium saucepan with water and bring to a gentle simmer.

2. Break the eggs gently into the pan one at a time. Cook over a very low heat, with the water hardly bubbling, for 3–4 minutes, or until the whites are set and the yolks remain runny.

3. Meanwhile, place a small, non-stick frying pan over a medium heat. Add the bacon and dry fry for about 2–3 minutes on each side, until crispy.

4. Divide the avocado between two plates and season with the lemon juice, a little salt and lots of ground black pepper.

5. Drain the eggs with a slotted spoon and place on top of the avocado. Roughly chop the bacon and scatter over the eggs. Season with chilli flakes, if using, and a little more pepper. Serve immediately, with a few salad leaves, if you like.

Kipper with poached egg and spinach

SERVES
1

PREP
10
mins

COOK
3
mins

50g young spinach leaves
½ tsp olive oil
100g kipper fillet
   (without butter)
1 large egg, fridge-cold
sprinkling freshly snipped
   chives, to serve (optional)

COOK'S TIP

If the kippers come with butter, use ½ the pat (around 3.5g) to cook one serving and leave out the olive oil. The additional calories from the butter will be minimal.

We love kippers in our house and this is a really easy way to prepare them. It will boost your daily protein and keep you feeling full well into the day. Kippers are also a good source of heart-healthy omega-3.

1. Half fill a medium saucepan with water and bring to a simmer.

2. Meanwhile, place the spinach in a microwavable shallow bowl or plate and toss with the oil and a little ground black pepper. Top with the kipper fillet, skin-side down and cover with a second plate or microwave cover (with the vents closed). Cook on high for about 2 minutes. The spinach should be wilted but not watery and the kipper hot throughout. (If you don't have a microwave, cook the kipper according to the pack instructions and wilt the spinach with the oil in a frying pan for about 1 minute over a medium heat, stirring.)

3. As soon as the kipper begins its cooking time, carefully crack the egg into the saucepan of water. Reduce the heat so it is barely simmering and cook for about 3 minutes, or until the white is cooked but the yolk remains runny.

4. Lift the egg out of the water with a slotted spoon and place on top of the kipper. Season with ground black pepper and sprinkle with chives, if using, to serve.

Sardines with tomatoes on sourdough

SERVES | **PREP** | **COOK**
2 | **10** mins | **5** mins

2 thin slices wholemeal
    or seeded sourdough
    (each around 40g)
1 × 120g can sardines in olive
    oil, drained
1 heaped tsp capers, drained
    (optional)
8 cherry tomatoes, halved
large handful young spinach
    leaves or rocket
2 tsp extra-virgin olive oil
dash balsamic vinegar or
    Tabasco

This is a super-healthy store-cupboard staple –
and another great source of omega-3.

1. Preheat the grill to high and line the grill pan with foil.

2. Place the bread on the foil and grill it until lightly
browned on both sides; or use a toaster.

3. Mash the sardines roughly on to the toast and scatter
with the capers, if using. (Make sure you completely cover
the toast so it doesn't burn when it goes under the grill.)
Place the tomatoes on top and season with a little salt
and ground black pepper.

4. Place under the grill for about 2 minutes, or until
the sardines are hot and the tomatoes have softened.

5. Transfer to two plates and serve with the leaves
alongside, dressed with the oil and a little balsamic
vinegar or Tabasco, to taste.

One-pan breakfast

SERVES	PREP	COOK
2	**10** mins	**7** mins

1 tbsp olive or canola oil
2 rashers smoked back
    bacon, each rasher cut
    into 3–4 slices
6–8 chestnut (or button)
    mushrooms (around 100g),
    quartered, or halved if small
10 cherry tomatoes, halved
50g young spinach leaves
2 medium eggs

The occasional fry-up is an allowable treat and with these ingredients it won't expand your waistline. On a non-fast day, you could serve this with a thin slice of wholegrain toast.

1. Heat the oil in a large, non-stick frying pan, add the bacon and mushrooms and fry over a medium heat for 2 minutes, or until lightly browned.

2. Add the tomatoes and stir-fry for a further 2 minutes, or until the tomatoes soften.

3. Fold in the spinach and move the whole mixture to the side of the pan.

4. Gently crack the eggs into the cleared space, reduce the heat to low and cook for 2–3 minutes, or until lightly set.

5. Spoon the bacon, tomatoes and mushrooms on to two warmed plates and top with the eggs. Season with ground black pepper and serve immediately.

Soups
and Salads

Soups and salads are amongst the easiest
meals to prepare and a great way to up
your fibre intake. These recipes are ideal
for a fasting day when you want a lunch
or light supper ready in minutes.

| PER SERVING | **148cals** | PROTEIN **7g** | CARBS **12.5g** | FAT **6.5g** | FIBRE **6g**

White bean and cauliflower soup

SERVES **4**

PREP **10** mins

COOK **25** mins

1 tbsp olive oil
1 small cauliflower (around 500g), cut into 2–3cm chunks, including most of the stalk (around 350g prepared weight)
1 chicken or vegetable stock cube
1 × 400g can butter, cannellini or haricot beans, drained
sprinkling finely chopped fresh rosemary or chives, to serve (optional)

COOK'S TIP

This soup tastes great drizzled with a little extra-virgin olive oil for an additional 27cals per teaspoon.

A smooth and filling low-calorie soup, which will also support your microbiome and help reduce inflammation. On a non-fast day, serve this soup with a thin slice of wholegrain bread. You could also sprinkle with finely grated Parmesan, mature Cheddar and/or toasted seeds.

1. Heat the oil in a large saucepan over a medium heat and add the cauliflower. Cook gently for 5 minutes, stirring occasionally.

2. Add the stock cube to the pan and 900ml just-boiled water. Bring to a gentle simmer, cover with a lid and cook for 15 minutes, or until the cauliflower is very soft, stirring occasionally.

3. Remove from the heat, add half the beans and blitz with a stick blender or cool slightly and blend in a food processor until very smooth.

4. Add the remaining beans, a little extra water, if needed, and reheat gently, stirring occasionally. Season to taste with salt and ground black pepper and sprinkle with rosemary or chives, if using, to serve.

Celery, broccoli and Stilton soup

SERVES | **PREP** | **COOK**
4 | **15** mins | **25** mins

1 tbsp olive oil
1 large onion, peeled
    and roughly chopped
4 celery sticks, trimmed
    and sliced
1 chicken or vegetable
    stock cube
200g broccoli, cut into
    small florets
100g Stilton
small handful roughly
    chopped fresh parsley or
    chives, to serve (optional)

Thanks to the soluble and insoluble fibre in the onion, celery and broccoli, this richly flavoured green soup will give your healthy gut microbes a good boost and help support your immunity.

1. Heat the oil in a large saucepan, add the onion and celery and fry over a medium heat for 5 minutes, or until beginning to soften, stirring regularly.

2. Crumble in the stock cube and add 1 litre water. Bring to the boil, then reduce the heat and simmer for 10 minutes, stirring occasionally.

3. Add the broccoli and cook for a further 5 minutes, or until tender.

4. Remove the soup from the heat and blitz with a stick blender or cool slightly and blend in a food processor until smooth. Add all but 25g of the Stilton and return to a low heat. Stir until the cheese melts. Add a splash of water, if needed.

5. Season with plenty of ground black pepper and salt, to taste. (You may not need salt as the cheese is fairly salty.) Divide the soup between four warmed bowls and crumble the remaining cheese over the top. Sprinkle with parsley or chives, if using, to serve.

PER SERVING | **123cals** | PROTEIN **2.5g** | CARBS **4g** | FAT **9g** | FIBRE **6.5g**

Leek and celeriac soup

SERVES	PREP	COOK
4	**15** mins	**25** mins

3 tbsp olive oil
2 large leeks (around 360g),
   trimmed and cut into
   roughly 2cm slices
½ medium celeriac (around
   375g), well scrubbed and cut
   into roughly 2cm chunks
15g fresh root ginger, peeled
   and finely chopped
1 vegetable or chicken
   stock cube
small handful roughly
   chopped fresh parsley,
   to serve (optional)

COOK'S TIP

You can replace the
celeriac with parsnips,
or the leeks with onions.

A creamy comfort soup. Root veg, such as knobbly celeriac or turnip, last for ages in the fridge. Although root veg is quite starchy, the fibre in it is hugely beneficial. Include the skin whenever you can, as this contains most of the health-promoting nutrients.

1. Place the oil in a large saucepan and gently fry the leeks and celeriac over a medium heat for 5 minutes, or until the leeks are softened but not coloured, stirring regularly.

2. Add the ginger and cook for 1 minute more, stirring.

3. Crumble the stock cube over the top and add 800ml water. Bring to the boil, then reduce the heat and simmer for 15–20 minutes, or until the celeriac is very soft, stirring occasionally.

4. Remove from the heat and blitz with a stick blender, or let it cool slightly and blend in a food processor until smooth. Season with salt and ground black pepper and reheat gently, adding extra water to thin, if needed.

5. Sprinkle with parsley, if using, and season with ground black pepper, to serve.

| PER SERVING | **275cals** | PROTEIN **15.5g** | CARBS **26.2g** | FAT **10.3g** | FIBRE **8g**

Store-cupboard bean soup

SERVES 3 | **PREP 10** mins | **COOK 20** mins

1 tbsp olive oil
½ medium onion, peeled
  and finely chopped
1 tsp hot smoked paprika
½ tsp dried oregano or dried
  mixed herbs
1 × 400g can chopped tomatoes
1 × 400g can organic mixed
  beans in water, or any other
  canned beans, not drained
1 vegetable or chicken
  stock cube
100g full-fat live Greek
  yoghurt, to serve

COOK'S TIP

If you are not using
organic beans, which are
canned without firming
agents, drain the beans
in a sieve and rinse under
running water before
adding to the pan. Add
100ml water if you do this.

A delicious Mexican-inspired soup. On a non-fast day, you could top this with sliced avocado, chorizo and grated cheese. Alternatively, you could share the soup between 2 people instead of 3.

1. Heat the oil in a large non-stick saucepan, add the onion and gently fry over a low-medium heat for 5 minutes, or until softened and beginning to colour, stirring regularly. Add the paprika and oregano and cook for a few seconds more, stirring constantly.

2. Tip the tomatoes into the pan, fill the empty can with water and pour this on top. Add the beans and their water (see tip below) and crumble over the stock cube. Bring to a gentle simmer and cook for 10 minutes, stirring occasionally.

3. Season to taste with salt and ground black pepper. Ladle into warmed bowls and top with full-fat live Greek yoghurt to serve.

Creamy zucchini soup

SERVES
4

PREP
15
mins

COOK
20
mins

2 tbsp olive oil
3 medium zucchinis (around
    600g), trimmed and cut
    into 1.5–2cm chunks
1 medium onion, peeled
    and roughly chopped
2 tsp medium curry powder
15g fresh root ginger, peeled
    and grated
200ml full-fat coconut milk
1 vegetable or chicken
    stock cube
8–12 fresh mint leaves,
    roughly chopped,
    plus extra to serve

COOK'S TIP

If you like your soup
chunky, don't bother to
blitz it – just top with the
shredded mint to serve.

Here's a simple and delicious way to use up any large
zucchinis that you might have. The spice is very mild
but gives the soup a bit more zing. You could try
scattering a teaspoon of toasted seeds over the top for
an extra 30cals.

1. Heat the oil in a large, wide-based saucepan and fry
the zucchini chunks and onion over a medium heat for
10–15 minutes, or until well softened, stirring regularly.

2. Stir in the curry powder and ginger, and cook for
30 seconds. Pour in 500ml water and the coconut milk,
crumble over the stock cube and bring to a simmer.
Cook for 2–3 minutes, stirring regularly.

3. Remove from the heat and season to taste with salt and
ground black pepper. Add the mint to the pan and blitz with
a stick blender until smooth. If the soup is a little thick for
your taste, add a splash more water and warm through gently.

4. Ladle into warmed bowls and top with more fresh mint
and a little ground black pepper to serve.

PER SERVING | **69cals** | PROTEIN **12g** | CARBS **3.5g** | FAT **0.5g** | FIBRE **1.5g**

Miso soup with mushrooms and prawns

SERVES | **PREP** | **COOK**
1 | **5** mins | **5** mins

½ pak choi, leaves separated
  and washed
3 level tsp miso paste
  (around 15g)
1 medium closed cup
  mushroom, finely sliced
50g large cooked and peeled
  prawns, thawed if frozen
small pinch crushed dried
  chilli flakes (optional)
small handful roughly
  chopped fresh coriander
  leaves, to serve (optional)

COOK'S TIP

For a vegetarian
alternative, substitute
tofu for the prawns.

Almost instant and very low-calorie, this is a fast-day life-saver. It was one of the recipes I demonstrated in our Channel 4 series 'Lose a Stone in 21 Days'. Miso paste has a deliciously sweet, salty, slightly tangy flavour. The prawns add a good boost of protein and omega-3, along with other nutrients, including selenium (which most of us are lacking and is important for the immune system). You can add a handful of young spinach leaves or cooked greens as well. Simply add at the same time as the prawns. Miso soup kept Michael going on his early 5:2 fast days.

1. Slice the pak choi and place in a small saucepan with 250ml water.

2. Stir in the miso paste, add the sliced mushroom and bring to a simmer. Cook for 3–4 minutes, or until the pak choi is beginning to soften.

3. Add the prawns and cook for a further minute, or until the prawns are hot.

4. Remove from the heat, stir in the chilli and coriander, if using, and ladle into a deep bowl or large mug to serve.

PER SERVING | **206cals** | PROTEIN **10g** | CARBS **19g** | FAT **8g** | FIBRE **8g**

Harissa lentil and chickpea soup with spinach

SERVES	PREP	COOK
4	**5** mins	**20** mins

2 tbsp olive or canola oil

1 large onion, peeled and finely chopped

1 heaped tbsp harissa paste (around 15g)

1–2 tsp ground turmeric (optional)

1 × 400g can chopped tomatoes

1 × 250g sachet ready-cooked puy lentils (or 1 × 400g can lentils, drained)

1 × 400g can chickpeas, drained

150g young spinach leaves or 3 balls frozen leaf spinach

small handful roughly chopped coriander leaves, to serve (optional)

The lentils and chickpeas provide an excellent plant-based source of protein in this fragrant North African flavoured soup. It is enhanced by a dollop of live Greek yoghurt – add 20cals for each 15ml tablespoon of yoghurt you use.

1. Heat the oil in a large saucepan, add the onion and gently fry over a low heat for 5 minutes, or until softened, stirring regularly.

2. Add the harissa paste and turmeric, if using, and cook for 1 minute more, stirring.

3. Add the tomatoes, lentils, chickpeas and 600ml cold water. Bring to a simmer and cook for 10 minutes, stirring occasionally.

4. Stir in the spinach and cook for a further 1–2 minutes, or until well softened.

5. Season with salt and ground black pepper and ladle into warmed bowls. Sprinkle with coriander, if using, to serve.

easy ways
with salads and dressings

A simple salad is one of the easiest things to throw together when time is short. With a few basic ingredients and good-quality protein, you have the ideal low-calorie meal.

Build a healthy salad

SERVES 1

1. Any healthy salad starts with lettuce, tomatoes, cucumber and pepper, and feel free to add other non-starchy plant ingredients to your plate – extra salad leaves, such as baby leaf, watercress, endive, rocket or young spinach leaves, as well as chicory, radishes, onion, spring onion, celery, cress, young kale, mushrooms, fresh herbs and/or chilli.

2. To turn the salad into a nutritious light lunch, you'll need to add protein. Here are some examples – for more ideas see page 239:

100g cooked chicken breast (153cals)
100g cooked peeled prawns (70cals)
100g tuna in brine or water (113cals)
60g halloumi, sliced and fried in ½ tsp
  olive oil for 1–2 mins (220cals)
50g full-fat feta (124cals)
½ avocado (149cals)
30g plain mixed nuts (179cals)
100g cooked puy lentils (143cals)

3. Finally, add 1 tablespoon dressing.

Add your favourite dressing

1. Place 1 teaspoon Dijon or wholegrain mustard, 1 tablespoon balsamic vinegar and 5 tablespoons extra-virgin olive oil in a screw-top jar (a small jam jar is ideal) and season with a pinch of flaked sea salt and lots of ground black pepper.

2. Add one or two of the following (optional):

1 tbsp finely chopped fresh herbs, such as
  parsley, basil, coriander, dill
1 tbsp baby capers, finely chopped
1 small garlic clove, peeled and crushed
finely grated zest lemon or lime
pinch crushed dried chilli flakes
pinch dried mixed herbs

3. Fasten the lid and shake the dressing really well. Adjust the seasoning to taste. Keep in the fridge and use within 2–3 days. Serve 1 tablespoon of the dressing per person (102cals). Don't worry if the olive oil solidifies a little. Leave at room temperature for a short while or shake well.

Crunchy rainbow salad with cashews and ginger

SERVES **2** | **PREP** **20** mins | **COOK** **10** mins

60g plain cashews,
    roughly chopped
3 tbsp mixed seeds
    (around 30g)
250g red cabbage (around
    ½ small red cabbage),
    very finely sliced
2 medium carrots (each
    around 80g), trimmed, well
    washed and coarsely grated
½ yellow or red capsicum,
    deseeded and thinly sliced
2 spring onions, trimmed
    and thinly sliced
1 small eating apple (around
    90g), cored and thinly sliced

For the dressing
2 tbsp extra-virgin olive oil
1 tbsp mirin (rice wine)
    or dry sherry
1 tbsp dark soy sauce
1 tbsp cider vinegar
1 tsp finely grated fresh
    root ginger
2 good pinches crushed
    dried chilli flakes

This Thai-inspired, brightly coloured salad can be served immediately or put into lidded containers for a packed lunch (put the dressing in the container first and only toss the salad when you are ready to eat). Don't be put off by the number of ingredients; it's very easy to make and tastes utterly delicious.

1. Preheat the oven to 200°C/fan 180°C/Gas 6.

2. Scatter the nuts over a baking tray and roast for 5 minutes. Add the mixed seeds and roast for a further 3–5 minutes, or until the nuts and seeds are lightly toasted. Set aside. You don't have to toast the nuts and seeds, but they taste better if you do.

3. Whisk together all the dressing ingredients in a large bowl.

4. Add the cabbage, carrots, capsicums, spring onions and apple, and toss everything together. Sprinkle over the nuts and seeds to serve.

PER SERVING | **442cals** | PROTEIN **17g** | CARBS **6g** | FAT **36g** | FIBRE **1.5g**

Tomato and basil salad with whipped goat's cheese

SERVES **2** | **PREP** **10** mins

200g mixed tomatoes,
   halved or sliced if large
small handful fresh basil
   leaves, torn
125g soft rindless goat's cheese
2 tbsp extra-virgin olive oil
4 tbsp full-fat live Greek
   yoghurt (around 50g)
2 tbsp pine nuts (around 18g)
   or 20g walnut pieces,
   lightly toasted
a few drops balsamic vinegar,
   ideally the thick variety

Sweet and tangy with a nutty crunch, this makes an ideal light lunch or side dish. The more variety in the tomatoes – in terms of colour and size – the better this salad is for you.

1. Arrange the tomatoes and basil on two plates and season with a little flaked sea salt and lots of ground black pepper.

2. Place the goat's cheese in a bowl with 1 tablespoon of the olive oil and the yoghurt and beat well until light and creamy. Drop spoonfuls on to the two salads, then sprinkle with the toasted pine nuts or walnuts.

3. Drizzle with the rest of the olive oil and the balsamic vinegar just before serving.

COOK'S TIP

This salad goes well with the Wholemeal mini flatbreads on page 236.

Lentil, zucchini, feta and beetroot salad

SERVES 2 | **PREP** 10 mins | **COOK** 3 mins

2 tsp olive or canola oil
2 medium zucchinis (each around 175g), trimmed and cut into roughly 1.5cm chunks
1 × 400g can lentils, drained and rinsed
125g cooked baby beetroot, cut into roughly 1cm chunks
40g rocket, young spinach or mixed baby leaves
1 tbsp extra-virgin olive oil
juice ½ lemon or 2–3 tsp balsamic vinegar
100g feta, broken into small pieces

COOK'S TIP

Cooked beetroot seasoned with mild malt vinegar works well in this recipe – the kind you find in the fruit and veg department of the supermarket, rather than the vinegar-heavy pickled beetroot sold in jars.

A great way to use up leftover lentils, this also makes a fab packed lunch. We try to slip lentils into meals where we can, as they are such a great source of fibre and nutrients. They also help to keep you 'regular', which can be a challenge on fasting days! Tinned or from pouches are fine.

1. Heat the oil in a large, non-stick frying pan, add the zucchinis and fry over a medium heat for 2–3 minutes, or until just beginning to brown. You don't want them to go too soft.

2. Tip the zucchinis into a large bowl and leave to cool for about 15 minutes.

3. Add the lentils, beetroot and salad leaves to the cooked zucchinis, season with a little salt and lots of freshly ground black pepper. Drizzle with the extra-virgin olive oil and lemon juice or balsamic vinegar and toss together.

4. Divide the salad between two shallow bowls, season with a little more black pepper and serve topped with the feta.

Tuna, bean and roasted capsicum salad

SERVES 4 | **PREP 10** mins

100g young spinach or mixed salad leaves

1 × 400g can mixed beans in water, drained and rinsed

1 × 280g jar roasted or char-grilled capsicums in oil, drained (around 170g drained weight), cut into roughly 2cm pieces

2 × 110g cans tuna steak in water or brine, drained

½ small red onion, peeled and cut into thin rings

2 tbsp extra-virgin olive oil

juice 1 small lemon

I knocked this up for lunch in minutes on a recent surfing holiday in Devon – mainly from jars and tins from the local shop. Our hungry surfers loved it, as did we. If you aren't serving four, simply halve the ingredients; or double them up for a crowd.

1. Scatter the spinach leaves over a large platter or into a wide salad bowl and top with the beans and capsicums. Toss very lightly together.

2. Flake the tuna on top of the salad, add the red onion, drizzle with the oil and lemon juice, season with lots of ground black pepper and serve.

COOK'S TIP

For extra flavour and omega-3, scatter a few anchovies over before the onion is added. You'll need roughly 8 anchovy fillets, drained and roughly chopped, which will add an extra 8cals per serving.

Prawn and pasta salad

SERVES **2** | **PREP** **10** mins | **COOK** **12** mins

40g wholewheat pasta,
   such as penne or fusilli
4 tbsp good-quality full-fat
   mayonnaise (around 50g)
½ tsp sweet paprika (optional)
1 tsp cider vinegar
200g cooked and peeled
   cold-water prawns
25g mixed salad leaves
½ × 195g can sweetcorn,
   drained, or 80g frozen
   sweetcorn, cooked
   and cooled
10 cherry tomatoes, halved
100g cucumber, cut into
   1.5cm chunks
¼ tsp crushed dried chilli
   flakes (optional)

COOK'S TIP

If making ahead, divide
the prawns between two
lidded containers and top
with the pasta, followed by
the sweetcorn, tomatoes,
cucumber and leaves. Keep
chilled and toss together
just before serving.

This salad contains a much smaller amount of pasta
than you might be used to but you will find it still tastes
great. This is also a very versatile dish so, if you don't
fancy prawns, use cooked chicken or ham instead – see
page 239; the prawns contain 70cals and 15.5g protein
per serving. Serve as a speedy lunch for two or layer
into lidded containers for an easy packed lunch.

1. Half fill a medium saucepan with cold water and bring to
the boil. Add the pasta, stir well and return to the boil. Cook
for 10–12 minutes, or according to the pack instructions,
until tender, stirring occasionally. Rinse the pasta under
cold running water, then drain well.

2. Mix the mayonnaise with the paprika, if using, and the
vinegar in a medium bowl. Stir in the prawns and season
with salt and ground black pepper.

3. Divide the salad leaves between two shallow bowls and
top with pasta, sweetcorn, tomatoes and cucumber. Spoon
over the prawn mayo, season with a little ground black
pepper and chilli flakes, if using, and serve.

PER SERVING | **367cals** | PROTEIN **43g** | CARBS **5g** | FAT **19g** | FIBRE **3g**

Warm chicken and avocado salad

SERVES | PREP | COOK
2 | **15** mins | **25** mins

2 skinless chicken breast
   fillets (each around 150g)
2 slices Parma ham
   or prosciutto
2 Little Gem lettuces, trimmed
   and leaves separated
½ small avocado, peeled,
   stoned and sliced (around
   60g prepared weight)
12 cherry tomatoes, halved
1 heaped tbsp mixed seeds
   (around 12g)
5g grated Parmesan (optional)
4 tsp extra-virgin olive oil
2 tsp balsamic vinegar,
   ideally the thick variety

COOK'S TIP

If making without
the Parmesan, you can
reduce the calories by
11 per serving.

This is a popular go-to recipe in our family. Even better,
our children make it for us. It works just as well for
lunch or supper and is easy to double up. It's a great
meal to boost your protein levels and will keep you
feeling full for longer, too.

1. Preheat the oven to 200°C/fan 180°C/Gas 6 and line
a baking tray with non-stick baking paper or foil.

2. Season the chicken breasts on both sides with a little
salt and ground black pepper, then wrap each one with
a slice of Parma ham or prosciutto. Place on the baking
tray and roast for 20–25 minutes, or until cooked
through. Leave to rest for about 5 minutes.

3. Tear the lettuce leaves and divide between two
shallow bowls or plates and arrange the avocado
and tomatoes on top.

4. Slice the chicken breasts and place one on top of
each salad. Sprinkle with the mixed seeds and Parmesan,
if using. Drizzle with the oil and balsamic vinegar,
season with ground black pepper and serve.

Chorizo and bean salad

SERVES | PREP | COOK
2 | **10** mins | **2** mins

25g chorizo, skinned
   and roughly chopped
2 tbsp extra-virgin olive oil
1 × 400g can mixed beans in
   water, drained and rinsed
100g roasted red capsicums
   from a jar, drained and sliced
25g pitted olives, any colour,
   sliced
50g young spinach leaves
1 tbsp cider vinegar

COOK'S TIP

Roast your own capsicums by placing them on a baking tray lined with foil and cook under a hot grill for about 10 minutes, or until the skins are blistered and blackened, turning regularly. Leave until cool enough to handle, then strip off the blackened skins and cut the capsicums into strips, discarding the seeds. Two smallish capsicums will give enough roasted capsicum for this recipe.

A high-protein, Mediterranean-style salad with a boost of gut-friendly fibre. Choose the hard, cured chorizo, rather than the soft, cooking kind. Any beans or chickpeas work well; just make sure they are canned in water.

1. Place the chorizo in a small frying pan with 1 tablespoon of the oil and place over a medium heat. Cook for 2 minutes, or until it begins to release its fat and turn lightly brown, stirring regularly.

2. Meanwhile, mix the beans, capsicums, olives and spinach in a large bowl.

3. Remove the pan from the heat and stir in the remaining oil and the vinegar. Leave to sizzle for a few seconds, then scatter the chorizo and warm dressing over the salad and toss lightly.

4. Divide the salad between two shallow bowls or plates and serve while still warm and before the leaves wilt.

Avocado, crispy bacon and white bean salad

SERVES | **PREP** | **COOK**
2 | **10** mins | **5** mins

2 tbsp extra-virgin olive oil
2 rashers smoked back bacon
   (around 75g), thinly sliced
2 tbsp pine nuts
2 Little Gem lettuces, trimmed
   and leaves separated
½ × 400g can cannellini or
   haricot beans, drained and
   rinsed (123g drained weight)
½ small avocado, peeled,
   stoned and sliced (around
   60g prepared weight)
10 cherry tomatoes,
   halved or quartered
1 tbsp balsamic vinegar

Simple and delicious – and your microbiome will love it. On a non-fast day, use a whole avocado and twice the amount of pine nuts, or top with Parmesan shavings and serve with a slice of wholegrain sourdough bread.

1. Heat 1 teaspoon of the oil in a small non-stick frying pan, add the bacon and pine nuts and fry over a low-medium heat for 2–3 minutes, or until the bacon is lightly browned and beginning to crisp, stirring regularly.

2. Meanwhile, tear the lettuce leaves into pieces and divide between two shallow bowls. Scatter the beans, avocado and tomatoes on top. Season with a little ground black pepper.

3. Remove the frying pan from the heat, stir in the remaining olive oil and the balsamic vinegar. Allow to bubble for a few seconds then spoon over the salad to serve.

Light Bites

Everyone makes up their 800cals on a fasting day differently. The recipes in this chapter are great for when you want a light meal to help you through the middle of the day. And they can easily be made in advance to be taken as a packed lunch to work.

PER SERVING | **287cals** | PROTEIN **15.5g** | CARBS **6g** | FAT **22g** | FIBRE **3g**

Low-carb Portobello 'pizzas'

SERVES **2** | PREP **10** mins | COOK **10** mins

2 tbsp extra-virgin olive oil, plus extra for greasing
2 garlic cloves, peeled and crushed
1 tsp dried oregano, plus some fresh oregano leaves (optional), to serve
4 Portobello or large flat mushrooms (each around 90g)
3–4 tbsp tomato purée
6–8 cherry tomatoes, sliced
100g ready-grated mozzarella

COOK'S TIP

Add extra protein by topping each mushroom with anchovy fillets, chorizo or salami. But don't forget to add the extra calories (see page 239).

This is adapted from a particularly popular recipe in our Fast 800 online programme. With a wide Portobello mushroom as a base and a delicious tomato and mozzarella topping, it has all the flavour of a traditional pizza but only a fraction of the calories.

1. Preheat the oven to 200°C/fan 180°C/Gas 6 and lightly grease a baking tray.

2. Mix the olive oil, garlic and oregano in a small bowl.

3. Place the mushrooms on the tray, stalk side up, and spread each one thickly with the tomato purée. Top with the sliced tomatoes and drizzle with the olive oil mixture. Sprinkle with the mozzarella and season with a little salt and plenty of ground black pepper. Bake for 8–10 minutes, or until the cheese is melted and has started to brown.

4. Serve sprinkled with fresh oregano leaves, if using, and lots of green vegetables or a large salad.

Easy frittata

SERVES	PREP	COOK
4	**10** mins	**30** mins

1 tsp olive oil, for greasing
6 spring onions, trimmed
   and finely sliced
125g roasted red capsicums
   from a jar, drained and
   thickly sliced
125g artichoke hearts from a
   jar, drained and quartered
100g Cheddar, coarsely grated
8 medium eggs

COOK'S TIP

You can use a shallow
ovenproof dish for this
recipe but you will need to
cook it for a little longer. Or
you could make individual
frittatas in greased ramekins
or individual pie dishes, but
you will need to reduce the
cooking time slightly.

A frittata makes an ideal lunch. The artichoke hearts
add a delicate flavour and lots of lovely gut-friendly
fibre. If you don't have any to hand, use extra capsicums,
or add a generous scattering of olives instead.

1. Preheat the oven to 200°C/fan 180°C/Gas 6 and
grease and line the base of a 20cm square cake tin
(not loose-based) with non-stick baking paper.

2. Place the spring onions, capsicums, artichoke hearts
and grated cheese in the tin and toss together lightly.

3. Whisk the eggs in a bowl and season with salt and
lots of ground black pepper. Pour on to the vegetables
and cheese and bake for 25–30 minutes, or until the
eggs are set and the frittata is slightly puffy and golden
brown. (Test by inserting the tip of a knife into the
centre – there should be no liquid remaining.)

4. Cut the frittata into squares and serve warm
or cold with a generous salad or lots of green veg.

Feta, pea and mint crustless quiche

SERVES 6 | **PREP** 10 mins | **COOK** 40 mins

1 tsp olive or canola oil,
    for greasing
200g feta, cut into roughly
    1.5cm cubes
200g frozen peas, thawed
4 spring onions, trimmed
    and finely sliced
6 large eggs
200g full-fat crème fraîche
1 heaped tbsp finely chopped
    fresh mint

COOK'S TIP

Quickly thaw the peas
by putting in a sieve and
pouring just-boiled water
slowly over the top.
Drain well.

This light and minty crustless quiche is lifted by
the salty feta. Perfect for a packed lunch, it will also
keep well in the fridge for up to two days. Serve warm
or cold with a lightly dressed mixed salad.

1. Preheat the oven to 200°C/fan 180°C/Gas 6 and
lightly oil a shallow round 20cm ceramic pie or quiche
dish. It should be around 4cm deep.

2. Arrange the cubes of feta and the peas in the dish
and sprinkle over the spring onions.

3. Beat the eggs and crème fraîche together in a bowl,
then stir in the mint and season well with ground black
pepper. (You probably won't need salt as the cheese
is salty already.)

4. Pour the egg mixture over the feta and peas
and bake for about 35–40 minutes, or until just set.
(Test by inserting the tip of a knife into the centre –
there should be no liquid remaining.)

5. Leave the quiche to cool for few minutes before
cutting into wedges to serve.

easy ways
with wraps

When time is short, or you are preparing a packed lunch, it is tempting to reach for the bread and make a sandwich, but the tricks here will give you fasting day solutions that are just as delicious and much better for you.

Use any of the protein-rich ingredients listed on page 239 with some non-starchy veg (see page 240) or mixed leaves, and fill one of the basic wraps listed below. If you have the calories spare, try adding a sauce or dressing (see page 61) or one of the dips on pages 90–1.

Build a lettuce wrap

SERVES 1
1 Little Gem lettuce

1. Remove 3–4 outer leaves and set them aside to provide the cups.

2. Slice the smaller leaves and place in a medium bowl, along with the filling ingredients of your choice. Season with salt and ground black pepper and mix well.

3. Spoon the filling into the lettuce cups and serve.

Build a nori wrap

SERVES 1
1 sheet dried nori, around 20cm square (5cals)
75g cooked and cooled brown rice (122cals)

1. Combine the filling ingredients of your choice (to make 80g filling).

2. Place the nori sheet on a board, shiny side down, and spread the rice almost all the way over it. Press down lightly with the back of a spoon.

3. Spoon the filling in a line across the centre of the rice.

4. Roll the nori firmly around the filling, using two hands. Trim the edges then cut into six pieces.

Build an omelette wrap

SERVES 1
1 large egg (78cals)
½ tsp olive or canola oil (14cals)

1. Beat the egg in a small bowl until smooth. Season with ground black pepper.

2. Brush a non-stick pan (the base no larger than around 19cm) with the oil and place over a medium heat.

3. Pour the egg into the pan and swirl so that it spreads around to completely cover the base. Cook for 1–2 minutes or until set.

4. Loosen with a spatula then flip and cook for 10 seconds more. Turn out on to a board and leave to cool for a few minutes.

5. Spread the egg wrap with your filling and roll up firmly. Cut in half diagonally to serve.

PER SERVING | **362cals** | PROTEIN **28g** | CARBS **22g** | FAT **16.3g** | FIBRE **9g**

Chinese-style egg-fried cauli-rice

SERVES **1** | PREP **10** mins | COOK **3** mins

2 medium eggs
3 tsp dark soy sauce
1 tsp canola oil
100g frozen edamame or peas
200g cauliflower florets,
    coarsely grated
    (see page 208)

1. Beat the eggs and 1 teaspoon of the soy sauce in a small bowl.

2. Heat the oil in a large non-stick frying pan or wok over a medium heat. Pour the egg into the pan and swirl around the base. Count slowly to 10, until it is just beginning to set, then stir into flaky chunks.

3. Add the frozen edamame or peas and cauliflower then stir-fry together for 2–3 minutes, until hot.

4. Season with the remaining soy sauce, tip into a warmed bowl and serve.

PER SERVING | **323cals** | PROTEIN **25g** | CARBS **16.5g** | FAT **16g** | FIBRE **7g**

Lightly curried cauli-rice

SERVES **1** | PREP **10** mins | COOK **3** mins

1 tsp canola oil
2 medium eggs, beaten
1 tsp medium curry powder
50g frozen peas or edamame
8 cherry tomatoes, halved
200g cauliflower florets,
    coarsely grated
    (see page 208)
lime wedge, to serve (optional)

1. Heat the oil in a large non-stick frying pan or wok over a medium heat. Pour the egg into the pan and swirl around the base. Count slowly to 10, until it is just beginning to set, then stir into flaky chunks.

2. Add the curry powder, frozen peas or edamame, tomatoes and cauliflower and stir-fry together for 2–3 minutes, until hot.

3. Tip into a warmed bowl and serve with a squeeze of fresh lime, if you like.

PER SERVING | **141cals** | PROTEIN **3.5g** | CARBS **3.2g** | FAT **11.6g** | FIBRE **4.8g**

Baba Ganoush

SERVES | PREP | COOK
4 | **10** mins | **35** mins

2 medium eggplants
(each around 275g)
2 large garlic cloves, peeled
and each cut into 4 slices
2 tbsp extra-virgin olive oil
2 tbsp tahini (around 35g)
1 tbsp fresh lemon juice
or ½ tbsp cider vinegar
1 tsp ground cumin

COOK'S TIP

For a more smoky flavour,
sprinkle with a little hot
or sweet smoked paprika
to serve.

A luxurious, garlicky eggplant dip, which works well as
a side dish, too. On a non-fast day, serve with toasted
wholemeal pitta bread or wholegrain sourdough.

1. Preheat the oven to 220°C/fan 200°C/Gas 7.

2. Cut the eggplants in half lengthways and score the
flesh deeply with a sharp knife, without cutting all the way
through to the skin. Place on a baking tray, cut side up.

3. Divide the garlic slices between the eggplant halves,
pressing them deeply into the flesh, making sure they
don't stick out or they may burn. Brush the eggplants
generously with 1 tablespoon of the oil and season well.
Bake for 35–40 minutes, or until golden brown and soft.

4. Remove from the oven and leave for 5–10 minutes,
or until cool enough to handle. Scoop the flesh and garlic
from two of the eggplant halves into a food processor
and discard the skin. Add the remaining olive oil, tahini,
lemon juice or vinegar and cumin. Blitz until smooth.

5. Add the remaining eggplant flesh to the blender
and blitz until just combined with the purée, but with
plenty of texture remaining – or for longer if you prefer
a smoother finish. Season to taste and serve drizzled
with a little extra olive oil, if you like, but don't forget
to add 27cals for each teaspoon.

Tzatziki

SERVES **6** | **PREP** **5** mins

½ large cucumber, coarsely grated
250ml full-fat live Greek yoghurt
1 heaped tbsp finely chopped fresh mint leaves
1 large garlic clove, peeled and crushed
¼ tsp sumac or paprika (optional)

Serve this dip with grilled chicken, vegetable sticks or as part of a meze with hummus, olives and other dips.

1. Place the cucumber in a large bowl with the yoghurt, mint and garlic. Season with a little salt and ground black pepper and mix thoroughly. Cover and chill for 30 minutes to allow the flavours to mingle, if you have time.

2. Serve sprinkled with the sumac or paprika, if using.

PER SERVING | **95cals** | PROTEIN **3.5g** | CARBS **1g** | FAT **8.5g** | FIBRE **1g**

Avocado and feta dip

SERVES **4** | **PREP** **5** mins

1 medium avocado (around 150g), peeled and stoned
1 small garlic clove, peeled and crushed
75g feta
juice ¼ lemon
pinch crushed dried chilli flakes, to serve (optional)

This dip makes a delicious light lunch. It is best eaten on the day it is made.

1. Mash the avocado thoroughly in a bowl. Add the garlic, feta and lemon juice, to taste, and season with a little salt and lots of ground black pepper. Mix thoroughly.

2. Transfer to a clean bowl and serve sprinkled with chilli flakes, if using, and lots of vegetable crudités for dipping.

UNDER 200 CALORIES

PER SERVING | 186cals | PROTEIN 13.5g | CARBS 2g | FAT 14g | FIBRE 0g

Smoked salmon pâté

SERVES 2 | PREP 5 mins

100g smoked salmon, finely chopped
75g full-fat soft cheese
1 tsp fresh lemon juice
assorted vegetable sticks, such as celery or carrots, cauliflower florets or sliced zucchini

This is a great way to use up smoked salmon that might be left over from another dish – and much better value than any shop-bought pâté!

1. Place the salmon, cheese and lemon juice in a bowl. Season with ground black pepper and mix together thoroughly.

2. Spoon into a small dish and serve with raw vegetable sticks or spread onto thin slices of zucchini as low-carb 'blinis'.

Smoky kale crisps

SERVES | **PREP** | **COOK**
2 | **5** mins | **6** mins

125g fresh kale, tough
   stalks removed and any
   large leaves torn into
   smaller pieces
1 tbsp olive oil
½ tsp smoked paprika,
   sweet or hot

COOK'S TIP

The kale can easily
overcook and become
browned, so watch it
carefully for the last
couple of minutes, as
ovens vary. You want
it crispy and still green.

A simple, fibre-rich alternative to a packet of crisps.
If you don't have paprika to hand, toss the kale with the
oil and 1 tablespoon of soy sauce, but leave out the salt.

1. Preheat the oven to 200°C/fan 180°C/Gas 6.

2. Place the kale in a bowl and toss thoroughly with
the oil, paprika and a couple of pinches of fine sea salt.

3. Scatter over a large baking tray and roast for 4 minutes.

4. Remove from the oven and turn the kale, then roast
for a further 2–3 minutes, or until crisp in places but
not burnt. The kale will continue to crisp up as it cools.

5. Leave to cool on the tray, then transfer to a bowl
and serve.

| PER SERVING | **72cals** | PROTEIN **4g** | CARBS **2.5g** | FAT **5g** | FIBRE **0.5g**

Smoked salmon 'sandwiches'

SERVES **2** | **PREP** **5** mins

A sliver of smoked salmon with a dollop of creamy horseradish sandwiched between two thin slices of cucumber – delicious.

30g full-fat soft cheese
1 tsp horseradish sauce
5cm cucumber, cut into
  12 × 3mm slices
25g smoked salmon,
  cut into small pieces

1. Mix the cheese and horseradish in a small bowl.

2. Arrange half the cucumber slices on a plate. Spread with the cheese mixture.

3. Divide the smoked salmon between the cucumber slices. Season with a little ground black pepper, then top with the remaining cucumber slices to serve.

UNDER **200** CALORIES | PER SERVING | **141cals** | PROTEIN **4g** | CARBS **12g** | FAT **8g** | FIBRE **2g**

Apple with peanut butter

SERVES **1** | **PREP** **5** mins

An irresistible combination – the tart, juicy apple and rich, crunchy peanut butter make a surprisingly healthy mouthful.

1 small apple (around 90g)
1 tbsp crunchy unsweetened
  peanut butter (around 15g)
pinch ground cinnamon,
  to serve (optional)

1. Cut the apple into quarters, remove the core and cut each quarter into 4 pieces.

2. Mix the peanut butter with 1–2 teaspoons water in a small bowl to thin for dipping.

3. Serve the apple wedges spinkled with the cinnamon, if using, and the peanut butter dip alongside.

PER SERVING | **110cals** | PROTEIN **2g** | CARBS **6g** | FAT **8g** | FIBRE **1.5g**

UNDER **200** CALORIES

Apple 'blinis'

SERVES
2

PREP
5
mins

1 medium apple (around 130g)

2 tbsp full-fat soft cheese or goat's cheese (around 25g)

10g jalapeño or piquant peppadew peppers from a jar, drained and roughly chopped

6 walnut halves (around 15g), roughly broken

Slices of apple make a fantastic base for cheese and nuts. Enjoy the sweet and piquant flavours in one bite. So simple to make and completely scrumptious.

1. Top and tail the apple then cut into thin slices, 3–4mm each, removing any pips (you can also remove the core, if you prefer).

2. Spread the apple slices with the soft cheese and arrange on a plate. Top with the peppers and walnuts, season with a good grinding of black pepper and serve.

PER SERVING | **137cals** | PROTEIN **3.5g** | CARBS **8g** | FAT **9.5g** | FIBRE **2.5g**

UNDER **200** CALORIES

Pear 'blinis'

SERVES
2

PREP
5
mins

1 medium pear (around 130g)

2 tablespoons soft blue cheese (around 25g), such as Dolcelatte

6 pecan nut halves (around 15g), roughly broken

These blinis are wonderfully versatile – try them with a different cheese or a sprinkling of seeds, instead of nuts.

1. Top and tail the pear then cut into thin slices, 3–4mm each, removing any pips (you can also remove the core, if you prefer).

2. Spread the pear slices with the blue cheese and arrange on a plate. Top with the pecans and serve.

Fish and Shellfish

We know fish is hugely good for us, loaded as it is with nutrients, such as vitamin D and protein. Oily fish, like mackerel, also provide an excellent source of omega-3. And yet many of us, including Michael until recently, assume fish is dull and fiddly to cook. Now he's a convert, not only enjoying the feisty dishes, but also appreciating the more delicate flavours.

Sweet chilli salmon with edamame

SERVES	PREP	COOK
2	**5** mins	**5** mins

1 tbsp olive or canola oil

200g frozen edamame, baby broad beans or peas

1 × 320–350g pack stir-fry vegetables

160g sweet chilli hot smoked salmon, or any hot smoked or poached salmon, skin removed, flaked into large chunks

1 tbsp dark soy sauce, to serve

dash sriracha or Tabasco (optional), to serve

COOK'S TIP

You'll find edamame beans in the frozen food section of larger supermarkets – make sure you choose the ones that have already been podded.

This is incredibly easy to throw together – delicious comfort food with lots of flavour to lift the spirits. You also get a healthy blast of omega-3 fish oils. On a non-fast day, you could serve it with a small portion of wholewheat or soba noodles.

1. Heat the oil in a large frying pan or wok over a high heat. Add the edamame and cook for 1 minute, or until beginning to thaw. Add the mixed vegetables and stir-fry for 3 minutes.

2. Add the salmon to the pan and cook for 1–2 minutes, or until hot, turning everything gently to avoid breaking up the fish too much.

3. Serve in warmed bowls sprinkled with the soy sauce and sriracha or Tabasco, if using.

Pesto baked fish

SERVES	PREP	COOK
2	**10** mins	**30** mins

2 red or yellow capsicums,
   deseeded and thickly sliced
2 medium-large zucchinis,
   cut into 2–3cm chunks
1 large red onion, peeled
   and cut into 12 wedges
2 tbsp olive oil
2 × 130g skinless white
   fish fillets, such as cod
   or haddock
2 tbsp pesto
lemon wedges, to serve

COOK'S TIP

Fresh basil pesto from the
chiller cabinet has a much
better flavour than the jars.

Add a Mediterranean twist to your fish with this easy
one pan traybake. Michael has grown to love eating
fish through adding plenty of flavour to it.

1. Preheat the oven to 200°C/fan 180°C/Gas 6.

2. Place all the vegetables in a large baking tray or roasting
tin. Drizzle with the oil, season with salt and lots of ground
black pepper and toss together. Bake for 15 minutes.

3. Remove the tray from the oven and turn all the
vegetables. Place the fillets on top of the veg then spoon
the pesto over the fish. Return the tray to the oven and
roast for 15 minutes, or until the fish is cooked through
and the vegetables are lightly browned.

4. Serve with lemon wedges for squeezing.

Salmon burgers

SERVES **2** | PREP **15** mins | COOK **8** mins

2 × 120g skinless salmon fillets,
  cut into large chunks
15g bunch fresh coriander,
  leaves roughly chopped,
  plus extra to serve
1 garlic clove, peeled
  and finely grated
15g fresh root ginger,
  peeled and finely grated
2 tsp dark soy sauce or
  1 tsp Thai fish sauce
2 spring onions, trimmed
  and thinly sliced
1 medium red chilli,
  finely chopped, or ½–1 tsp
  crushed dried chilli flakes
2 tsp olive, coconut or
  canola oil
lime wedges, to serve

A simple fish burger that can be knocked up in very little time. Serve with some finely diced red chilli, if you like a bit more heat.

1. Put the salmon in a food processor with the coriander, garlic, ginger and soy or fish sauce. Season with lots of ground black pepper and blitz on the pulse setting until it comes together as a thick, slightly chunky paste. Don't allow it to become too smooth.

2. Remove the blade and stir the spring onions and chilli into the mixture. Form into two balls and flatten into burger shapes.

3. Heat the oil in a medium non-stick frying pan and fry the burgers over a moderate heat for 3–4 minutes on each side, or until golden brown and cooked through.

4. Serve with lime wedges and a mixed salad.

PER SERVING | **349cals** | PROTEIN **24g** | CARBS **8g** | FAT **24g** | FIBRE **3g**

Roasted fish with a cheese and parsley crumb

SERVES **2** | PREP **10** mins | COOK **27** mins

1 medium zucchini, cut into roughly 1.5cm chunks
120g roasted red capsicums from a jar, drained and roughly sliced
2 tsp extra-virgin olive oil
2 sea bream or sea bass fillets (each around 90g)

For the topping
20g wholegrain sourdough bread, blitzed into breadcrumbs
20g mature Cheddar, coarsely grated
few sprigs fresh parsley, leaves finely chopped
finely grated zest ¼ lemon, plus extra lemon wedges, to serve

COOK'S TIP

We keep sliced sourdough in the freezer, so we can turn it into toast or crumbs any time.

This is a simple way to cook fish and an easy introduction if it's not something you prepare often. If you don't have fresh parsley, use frozen, or finely sliced spring onions instead.

1. Preheat the oven to 200°C/fan 180°C/Gas 6.

2. Place the zucchini and roasted capsicum pieces in a small baking tray, drizzle over the oil, season with black pepper and toss together lightly. Roast for 15 minutes.

3. Meanwhile, mix the breadcrumbs, cheese, parsley and lemon zest together in a small bowl to make the topping. Season with a little salt and lots of ground black pepper.

4. Remove the tray from the oven and turn the zucchini and capsicum pieces. Place the fish fillets on the vegetables, skin-side down, and sprinkle the breadcrumb mixture on top of the fish.

5. Bake for about 12 minutes, or until the fish is cooked and the crumbs are lightly browned.

6. Serve with lots of green vegetables or a large mixed salad and extra lemon wedges for squeezing over.

| PER SERVING | **250cals** | PROTEIN **12g** | CARBS **11g** | FAT **17g** | FIBRE **1g**

Smoked mackerel fishcakes

SERVES **4** | PREP **10** mins | COOK **11** mins

4 tsp olive or canola oil
1 small leek (around 140g), trimmed and finely sliced
180g smoked mackerel fillets, skin removed
60g full-fat soft cheese
2 tsp capers, drained, or pickled jalapeño peppers, drained and roughly chopped (optional)
50g wholegrain bread or sourdough, blitzed into breadcrumbs
lemon wedges, to serve (optional)

These well-flavoured fishcakes were introduced to us by our son Dan when he was recovering from coronavirus.

1. Heat 2 teaspoons of the oil in a non-stick frying pan, add the leeks and gently fry over a low heat for about 5 minutes, or until very soft, stirring regularly. Tip into a mixing bowl and leave to cool for 15 minutes.

2. Flake the mackerel into the bowl, add the cheese, capers or jalapeños, if using, and breadcrumbs. Season with plenty of ground black pepper (unless using peppered mackerel) and mix together thoroughly with a fork. Form the mackerel mixture into four balls and flatten into fishcakes.

3. Heat the remaining oil in the same frying pan over a medium heat. Cook the fishcakes for 2–3 minutes on each side, or until lightly browned and hot through. Don't move them about too much as they are fairly delicate and could break apart.

4. Serve warm with a lemon wedge and a green salad, or cold as part of a packed lunch.

Quick fish curry

SERVES | **PREP** | **COOK**
4 | **10** mins | **20** mins

1 tbsp coconut or canola oil

1 medium onion, peeled and thinly sliced

1 yellow capsicum, deseeded and cut into roughly 2cm chunks

2–3 tbsp medium Indian curry paste, such as tikka masala or rogan josh

1 × 400g can chopped tomatoes

100g green beans, trimmed and halved, or frozen green beans

500g frozen, skinless white fish fillets, such as cod or haddock

small handful freshly chopped coriander (optional)

COOK'S TIP

You can use salmon instead but you will need to increase the calories to 375 per serving. If using fresh fish, rather than frozen, cook for just 5–6 minutes, turning after 3 minutes.

I love the way the frozen fish in this recipe is placed on top of the curry sauce and delicately steamed, absorbing the curry flavours. On a non-fast day, serve with freshly cooked brown rice.

1. Heat the oil in a large, deep non-stick frying pan. Add the onion and capsicum and fry over a low-medium heat for 5 minutes, or until softened, stirring regularly. Add the curry paste and cook for 1 minute more.

2. Stir in the tomatoes, then refill the empty can with water and add this to the pan (you'll need around 400ml). Bring to a gentle simmer and stir in the green beans. Season with salt and ground black pepper to taste.

3. Place the frozen fish fillets on top of the sauce – there is no need to thaw them first – and cover the pan with a lid. Simmer gently, without stirring, for 5 minutes.

4. Turn the fish and cook for a further 5 minutes, or until the fish is cooked and hot through. The timing will depend on how thick the fillets are, but you can tell when they are ready as they will begin to break apart when prodded gently with a fork.

5. Sprinkle with freshly chopped coriander, if using, and serve with leafy green veg and portions of cauli-rice (see page 208).

Seed-crusted baked fish

SERVES 2 | **PREP** 15 mins | **COOK** 15 mins

2 tbsp mixed seeds
2 tbsp flaked almonds
1 tbsp olive oil
2 × 120g thick, skinless
    white fish fillets, such
    as cod or haddock
lemon wedges, to serve

For the lemon mayo
finely grated zest ½
    small lemon
1½ tbsp good-quality
    mayonnaise (around 20g)
2 tbsp full-fat live
    Greek yoghurt

COOK'S TIP

Serve with the celeriac chips on page 150 for an extra 64cals.

This is Justine's version of battered fish and tastes utterly delicious. Instead of using a stodgy batter, she coats the fish with mixed seeds as a high-protein, low-carb alternative.

1. Preheat the oven to 200°C/fan 180°C/Gas 6 and line a baking tray with non-stick baking paper.

2. Mix the lemon mayo ingredients together in a small bowl and set aside for the flavours to mingle.

3. Place the seeds and almonds in a pestle and mortar, add a good pinch of salt and plenty of ground black pepper and pound to a coarse powder – it doesn't need to be too fine. You can also do this in a spice grinder or with a stick blender. Sprinkle the powder over a large plate. Drizzle the oil over a second plate.

4. Place each piece of fish in the oil and turn to coat lightly, then transfer to the seed mix and press firmly on both sides. Place the fillets on the lined tray and bake for about 15 minutes, or until the fish is beginning to flake and the seeds are lightly browned.

5. Divide between two warmed plates and serve with the mayonnaise, lemon wedges for squeezing and plenty of non-starchy veg or a large salad.

Tuna Provençal

SERVES **2** | **PREP** **5** mins | **COOK** **5** mins

2 tsp extra-virgin olive oil, plus 1 tbsp

2 × 115g fresh tuna steaks, thawed if frozen

40g slow-roasted tomatoes (semi-dried) from a jar or tub, drained and roughly chopped

10 pitted black olives (around 30g), ideally kalamata, halved

1 tbsp fresh lemon juice

small handful roughly chopped fresh parsley, to serve (optional)

Fresh tuna steak is surprisingly filling and packed with protein. Here, we pan-fry it and serve it alongside a punchy tomato and olive sauce. Anyone not following the Fast 800 can add a small portion of new potatoes.

1. Heat the 2 teaspoons oil in a medium frying pan over a medium heat. Season the tuna on both sides with a little salt and plenty of coarsely ground black pepper. Add to the pan and cook for 2 minutes.

2. Turn the tuna and add the tomatoes, olives, the remaining oil and lemon juice to the pan. Cook for a further 1–2 minutes, or until tuna is cooked to taste, and crushing the tomatoes and olives together to make a loose sauce.

3. Divide the tuna between two plates and spoon the tomato and olive sauce over the top. Sprinkle with the parsley, if using, and serve with salad or freshly cooked green beans.

Simple fish stew

SERVES | PREP | COOK
4 | **15** mins | **25** mins

1 tbsp olive oil
½ medium onion, peeled
   and thinly sliced
1 medium fennel bulb,
   trimmed, halved
   lengthways and thinly
   sliced, any fronds reserved
2 garlic cloves, peeled and
   very thinly sliced
1 tsp ground coriander
1 × 400g can chopped tomatoes
2 tbsp tomato purée
300g skinless white fish fillets,
   such as cod or haddock,
   cut into 2–3cm chunks
200g cooked peeled prawns,
   thawed if frozen
finely pared or grated zest
   1 small lemon
15g bunch fresh flat-leaf
   parsley, leaves roughly
   chopped

The delicate flavour of the fennel in this recipe really complements the fish. You can use any white fish but the thicker fillets are better. On non-fast days, you could serve with some brown rice, quinoa or a slice of warmed wholegrain bread and top with garlic mayonnaise.

1. Heat the oil in a large wide-based saucepan or flameproof casserole. Add the onion and fennel, cover with a lid and fry over a low-medium heat for 8 minutes, or until the fennel is beginning to soften, stirring occasionally.

2. Stir in the garlic and coriander and cook for 1 minute, then add the tomatoes and tomato purée, along with 400ml water. Season with a little salt and ground black pepper and bring to a simmer.

3. Reduce the heat, cover loosely with a lid and cook for 5 minutes, stirring occasionally. Remove the lid and simmer for a further 5–6 minutes, or until the fennel is almost soft and the liquid has reduced, stirring regularly.

4. Stir in the fish, then simmer gently for 2–3 minutes. Scatter the prawns on top and cook for a further 1–2 minutes, or until the fish is cooked and the prawns are hot.

5. Combine the lemon zest and parsley in a small bowl and scatter over the top, along with any reserved fennel fronds. Serve with lots of green beans or long-stemmed broccoli.

PER SERVING | **271cals** | PROTEIN **21.5g** | CARBS **16g** | FAT **12.5g** | FIBRE **4g**

Prawn zoodles and spaghetti with chilli and lemon

SERVES **2** | PREP **10** mins | COOK **12** mins

40g dried wholewheat
  spaghetti
1 large zucchini, trimmed
  and spiralized or peeled
  into ribbons, or use a pack
  of zoodles
2 tbsp extra-virgin olive oil
200g cooked, peeled prawns,
  thawed if frozen and drained
2 garlic cloves, peeled and
  crushed or finely grated
1–1½ tsp crushed dried
  chilli flakes
finely grated zest and juice
  1 small lemon

Prawns, lemon and chilli are generally a winning combination. Here we have swapped in some zoodles, so you get the luxurious feel of pasta but with far fewer calories.

1. Half fill a large pan with water and bring to the boil. Add the pasta and cook according to the pack instructions. Stir in the zoodles for the last 15–20 seconds of the cooking time. Drain the pasta and zoodles in a colander and set aside.

2. Meanwhile, heat the oil in a large pan, add the prawns, garlic and chilli and fry over a medium heat for about 2 minutes, or until heated through, stirring regularly. Don't overcook the prawns or they will toughen.

3. Add the spaghetti and zoodles, lemon zest and juice to the pan. Toss together well, season with salt and plenty of ground black pepper and serve in warmed bowls.

COOK'S TIP

You can use raw prawns but you will need to cook them for 1–2 minutes before adding the chilli and garlic. They should be hot and pink throughout before tossing with the spaghetti and zoodles.

PER SERVING | **291cals** | PROTEIN **22.5g** | CARBS **19g** | FAT **13g** | FIBRE **4g**

Crab spaghetti and zoodles

SERVES **2** | **PREP** **10** mins | **COOK** **12** mins

40g dried wholewheat
   spaghetti
2 tbsp olive oil
1 garlic clove, peeled
   and finely chopped
4 anchovy fillets in olive oil,
   drained and finely chopped
8 cherry tomatoes, halved
2 tbsp cider vinegar
1 × 145g can white crabmeat,
   drained, or cooked white
   fresh crabmeat
15g bunch fresh parsley, leaves
   and stalks finely chopped
1 large zucchini (around 285g),
   trimmed and spiralized or
   peeled into ribbons, or use a
   pack of zoodles
pinch crushed dried chilli
   flakes, to serve (optional)

A quick, simple supper that is relatively low in carbs. Crab, with its delicate, sweet taste, is a high-protein gem, rich in iron, zinc, magnesium and anti-inflammatory omega-3.

1. Half fill a large pan with water and bring to the boil. Add the pasta and cook according to the pack instructions.

2. Five minutes before the spaghetti is ready, heat the olive oil in a large frying pan over a medium heat. Add the garlic, anchovies and tomatoes and cook for 30 seconds, stirring constantly, until the anchovies break up. Add the vinegar and simmer for 1 minute before stirring in the crabmeat and parsley. Cook together for 1–2 minutes.

3. To cook the zoodles, add to the saucepan with the pasta for the final 15–20 seconds of the cooking time, then immediately drain in a colander.

4. Tip the spaghetti and zoodles into the pan with the crab, season with a generous twist of black pepper, sprinkle with chilli flakes, if using, and toss together for 1–2 minutes before serving.

Adrian's prawn and egg curry

SERVES | PREP | COOK
2 | **10** mins | **25** mins

2 large eggs
1 tbsp olive or canola oil
1 tsp cumin seeds
1 medium onion, peeled
   and finely chopped
1 tbsp medium curry powder,
   or more to taste
2 garlic cloves,
   peeled and crushed
15g fresh root ginger,
   peeled and finely grated
1 × 400g can chopped tomatoes
200g cooked peeled prawns,
   thawed if frozen
small handful freshly
   chopped coriander,
   to serve (optional)

COOK'S TIP

Top with sliced green
chilli for some extra heat.

This recipe comes from Adrian, one of the brilliant
volunteers in our Channel 4 series 'Lose a Stone in
21 Days'. It is a favourite in his family, who like their
curries really spicy, so we've simplified it a bit and
made it less fiery.

1. Half fill a medium pan with water and bring to the boil.
Add the eggs, return to the boil and cook for 8 minutes.
Rinse under running water until cold.

2. Meanwhile, heat the oil in a deep, large non-stick frying
pan. Add the cumin seeds and fry over a medium heat for
20–30 seconds, stirring. Add the onion and fry for 5 minutes,
or until softened and beginning to colour, stirring regularly.

3. Sprinkle over the curry powder, garlic and ginger, and
cook for 1 minute, stirring constantly. Stir in the tomatoes,
then fill the empty can with water and add this to the pan.
Bring to a gentle simmer and cook for 12–15 minutes,
stirring regularly.

4. Add the prawns and cook for about 1 minute, stirring
in an extra splash of water if the sauce looks very thick.

5. Meanwhile, remove the shells from the eggs and cut
them into quarters. Place them on top of the curry and
simmer gently for 1–2 minutes without stirring, or until
the prawns are hot and the eggs are warmed through.

6. Scatter with fresh coriander, if using, and serve with
cooked greens and cauli-rice (see page 208), if you like.

Thai-style mussels

SERVES 2 | **PREP** 15 mins | **COOK** 10 mins

1kg fresh live mussels

2 tsp coconut or canola oil

6 spring onions, trimmed
   and finely sliced

2 garlic cloves, peeled
   and finely sliced

15g fresh root ginger, peeled
   and very finely chopped

2 tbsp red or green Thai
   curry paste

4 fresh kaffir lime leaves
   or 6 dry kaffir lime leaves

200ml coconut milk

2 tsp Thai fish sauce

20g bunch fresh coriander,
   leaves roughly chopped

Fresh mussels are a favourite in our house. These ones are simmered in a delicious Thai-inspired coconut broth. Kaffir lime leaves really help lift the flavour, but if you can't find any, use 1 teaspoon of lime zest instead.

1. Scrub the mussels well, removing any feathery 'beards' and discarding any that are damaged or don't shut tight when gently tapped. Rinse in cold water and set aside.

2. Heat the oil in a large, non-stick frying or sauté pan with a lid. Add the spring onions, garlic and ginger and fry very gently over a medium heat for 1 minute, or until softened but not coloured, stirring regularly. Stir in the curry paste and lime leaves and cook for 1 minute more.

3. Pour in the coconut milk and stir in the fish sauce. Bring to a gentle simmer and cook for 2–3 minutes, or until the coconut milk is slightly thickened, stirring occasionally. Season with ground black pepper.

4. Increase the heat, add the mussels and coriander, cover the pan with a lid and cook for 3 minutes. Remove the lid, stir well, cover and cook for a further 3 minutes, or until all the mussels have steamed open and are thoroughly cooked.

5. Remove the pan from the heat and discard any mussels that haven't opened before serving in bowls with steamed greens on the side.

Chicken, Turkey and Duck

Poultry is perfect for a fasting day –
a source of high-quality protein, which
is also relatively low in calories. We have
included our own Fast 800 twists on
a range of classic dishes, from curries
and stir-fries to a good old roast.

| PER SERVING | **246cals** | PROTEIN **36g** | CARBS **11.5g** | FAT **4.5g** | FIBRE **8g**

Simple roast chicken with mixed green veg

SERVES	PREP	COOK
4	**10** mins	**80** mins

1.6kg whole chicken
1 small lemon, quartered
½ tsp dried thyme or 2 tsp
   fresh thyme leaves

For the green veg
300g frozen peas
1 head broccoli, cut into
   small florets
2 slender leeks, trimmed
   and cut into 1.5cm slices
50g kale, spring green or
   cabbage leaves, trimmed
   and thickly shredded

COOK'S TIP

Any leftover chicken
can be served cold in
a salad the next day.

Yes, you can still enjoy a classic roast chicken. We've created a lighter, slightly lemony gravy to go with it and it's served with lots of lovely green vegetables.

1. Preheat the oven to 200°C/fan 180°C/Gas 6.

2. Place the chicken in a roasting tin, with the lemon pieces inside. Season well with salt and ground black pepper and sprinkle with the thyme. Roast for 1 hour 15 minutes, or until thoroughly cooked and the juices run clear.

3. Remove from the oven and transfer to a warmed platter. Cover with foil and leave to rest for 10 minutes.

4. Meanwhile, cook the vegetables. Third fill a large saucepan with water and bring to the boil. Add the peas and return to the boil. Add the remaining vegetables and cook for 2–3 minutes, or until tender. Drain everything in a colander, reserving the cooking water, then tip the vegetables into a warmed serving dish.

5. To make a simple gravy, spoon off and discard any fat floating on top of the chicken juices in the roasting tin, then place the tin on the hob over a medium heat. Add 3 tablespoons of the vegetable water and cook until bubbling, stirring to incorporate any sediment from the bottom of the pan. Pour the gravy carefully into a warmed jug.

6. Carve the chicken and serve around 120g per person, without skin, alongside the vegetables and with the gravy spooned over the top.

PER SERVING | **189cals** | PROTEIN **38.5g** | CARBS **1g** | FAT **3.5g** | FIBRE **0.5g**

Tarragon poached chicken

SERVES **4** | PREP **10** mins | COOK **20** mins

1 chicken stock cube
1 tsp dried tarragon
1 bay leaf (optional)
4 skinless chicken breast
   fillets (each around 150g)
6 tbsp full-fat live Greek
   yoghurt (around 75g)
4 tsp wholegrain mustard
1 garlic clove, peeled
   and crushed
15g bunch fresh parsley,
   leaves finely chopped

COOK'S TIP

When you slice the chicken, there should be no pinkness in the centre and the juices should run clear. If in any doubt, pop it back into the stock and cook for a little longer.

Having always assumed that poached chicken would be rather bland, I have recently discovered the joys of this flavourful and succulent way of cooking.

1. Place the stock cube, tarragon and bay leaf, if using, in a large saucepan and add 750ml water. Bring to a gentle simmer, stirring, until the stock dissolves.

2. Carefully lower the chicken breasts into the water and return to a slow simmer. Reduce the heat, cover loosely with a lid and simmer gently for 15–20 minutes, depending on the thickness of the breast, turning the chicken once, until thoroughly cooked (see Cook's Tip).

3. Remove from the heat and transfer the chicken to a board, cover loosely with foil and leave to rest for 5–10 minutes.

4. Place 2 tablespoons of the cooking liquid in a small bowl and mix with the yoghurt, mustard, garlic and nearly all the parsley and stir until thoroughly combined. Season with salt and ground black pepper.

5. Slice the chicken into pieces and arrange on a serving platter. Spoon over the sauce and scatter with the remaining parsley. Eat hot or cold with plenty of fresh green or coloured non-starchy veg.

Orange and rosemary chicken

SERVES **4** | **PREP** **15** mins | **COOK** **40** mins

2 medium red onions, peeled
   and each cut into 8 wedges
2 capsicums (1 red and
   1 yellow), deseeded and
   cut into 3cm chunks
2 medium zucchinis, trimmed,
   halved lengthways and cut
   into 2cm chunks
2 medium oranges, 1 quartered
   then quarters halved
   widthways, the other juiced
1 tsp dried rosemary or
   1 tbsp finely chopped
   fresh rosemary
2 tbsp extra-virgin olive oil
6 boneless, skinless chicken
   thighs (around 600g total
   weight), trimmed of fat
   and halved

Chicken thighs are the juiciest and tastiest parts of a chicken, in my view. Combine them with Mediterranean veg and citrus juices and you have an easy winner.

1. Preheat the oven to 200°C/fan 180°C/Gas 6.

2. Place the onions, capsicums, zucchinis, orange wedges and rosemary in a large roasting tin. Drizzle with 1 tablespoon of the oil, season with salt and ground black pepper and toss together lightly.

3. Nestle the chicken thighs amongst the vegetables and orange pieces. Drizzle over the orange juice and remaining oil. Season the chicken with salt and ground black pepper and roast for about 40 minutes, or until the chicken is thoroughly cooked and all the vegetables are tender and lightly browned.

4. Remove from the oven and serve with a crisp green salad.

| PER SERVING | **187cals** | PROTEIN **21.5g** | CARBS **12g** | FAT **5g** | FIBRE **5.5g**

Lemon chicken

SERVES **2** | **PREP** **10** mins | **COOK** **5** mins

1 tsp cornflour
1 tsp dark soy sauce
finely grated zest and juice
    ½ small lemon
2 tsp coconut or canola oil
1 skinless chicken breast fillet
    (around 150g), cut into
    1.5cm slices
1 capsicum, any colour,
    deseeded and sliced
1 medium carrot (around 80g),
    trimmed and thinly sliced
100g broccoli, cut into
    small florets
150ml chicken stock
    (made with ½ stock cube)
4 spring onions, trimmed
    and thickly sliced

COOK'S TIP

This can be made with firm tofu or prawns instead of chicken. Simply fry tofu with the vegetables in step two, or add prawns for the last couple of minutes of the cooking time.

A luscious, tangy stir-fry that makes two generous portions for very few calories. We tend to avoid cornflour in our recipes, but here it helps create a lovely glossy sauce to coat the chicken and vegetables. On a non-fast day, you could serve this with a few tablespoons of wholegrain rice.

1. Mix the cornflour with the soy sauce and lemon juice in a small bowl.

2. Heat the oil in a large frying pan or wok over a high heat, add the chicken, capsicum, carrot and broccoli and stir-fry for 2–3 minutes, or until the chicken is lightly browned and the vegetables are beginning to soften.

3. Pour the lemon and soy mixture into the pan, add the chicken stock and spring onions and bring to a simmer. Reduce the heat and cook for 2 minutes, or until the sauce is slightly thickened and the chicken is cooked through, stirring regularly.

4. Sprinkle with grated lemon zest and serve with cauli-rice (see page 208).

Pesto chicken traybake

SERVES **2** | PREP **15** mins | COOK **40** mins

1 medium red onion, peeled and cut into 10 wedges

2 capsicums, any colour, deseeded and cut into roughly 3cm chunks

1 medium zucchini, trimmed, halved lengthways and cut into roughly 2cm chunks

3 tsp extra-virgin olive oil

2 skinless chicken breast fillets (each around 150g)

2 tbsp sun-dried tomato pesto

½ tsp paprika, any kind (optional)

Delicious served hot or cold as a salad, this is a real favourite with Justine's family and a doddle to double up if you are feeding more. We use red, sun-dried tomato pesto but you could use green basil pesto instead, if you like.

1. Preheat the oven to 200°C/fan 180°C/Gas 6.

2. Place the onion, capsicums and zucchini in a large roasting tin. Drizzle with 2 teaspoons of the oil, season with salt and ground black pepper and toss together lightly. Roast for 10 minutes.

3. Meanwhile, place the chicken breasts on a board and cut each one horizontally through the middle so they can be opened out like a book. Spread with the pesto and close.

4. Remove the tray from the oven and turn all the veg. Nestle the chicken breasts amongst the vegetables, drizzle over the remaining oil and season with the paprika, if using, a little salt and lots of ground black pepper. Roast for 20–25 minutes, or until the chicken is cooked through and all the vegetables are tender and lightly browned.

5. Remove from the oven and serve with a crisp green salad or steamed leafy veg.

Garden chicken casserole

SERVES **4** | **PREP** **20** mins | **COOK** **60** mins

2 tbsp olive oil
6 boneless, skinless chicken
   thighs (around 600g total
   weight), trimmed of fat
   and quartered
1 large onion, peeled and
   finely sliced
3 medium carrots (around
   250g total weight), well
   washed, trimmed and
   cut into 1.5cm slices
275g swede, well scrubbed
   and cut into 2.5cm chunks
500ml chicken stock
   (made with 1 stock cube)
1 tsp mixed dried herbs
2 medium leeks, trimmed
   and cut into 1.5cm slices
100g frozen peas

A traditional, comforting casserole with delicate flavours. Chicken thighs are simmered in the oven with lots of lovely prebiotic vegetables, so it's not just your waistline that will approve, but your gut bacteria, too.

1. Preheat the oven to 200°C/fan 180°C/Gas 6.

2. Heat the oil in a medium flameproof casserole over a moderate heat. Add the chicken and onion, season with a little salt and lots of ground black pepper and fry for 6–8 minutes, stirring regularly, until the chicken is coloured on all sides and the onion is beginning to brown.

3. Add the carrots, swede, stock and herbs. Bring to a simmer then cover with a lid and transfer to the oven to cook for 30 minutes.

4. Remove from the oven and use a ladle to take out around 100ml liquid, including some carrots and swede, and either mash these in a small bowl or put them in a jug and blitz to a purée with a stick blender. Return this to the stew and stir it in to thicken the sauce.

5. Add the leeks and peas, cover again and return to the oven for a further 20–30 minutes, or until the chicken is tender.

6. Remove from the oven and serve with lightly cooked shredded cabbage or kale.

Tex-Mex chicken and bean bowls

SERVES **4** | PREP **15** mins | COOK **25** mins

1 tbsp olive oil
1 medium onion, peeled
　and finely chopped
2 capsicums, any colour,
　deseeded and sliced
4 skinless chicken breast
　fillets (600g total weight),
　cut into 2cm chunks
1–2 tbsp chipotle paste
　(see tip below)
1 × 400g can chopped tomatoes
1 × 400g can black beans or
　red kidney beans, drained
　and rinsed
1 chicken stock cube
200g full-fat live Greek
　yoghurt
small handful freshly chopped
　coriander, to serve

This is a high-protein meal with a smoky chipotle sauce that all the family will love. On a non-fast day, you could serve it with a small portion of brown rice, and avocado, cheese and soured cream on the side.

1. Heat the oil in a large non-stick frying pan, add the onion, capsicums and chicken and fry over a medium heat for 8–10 minutes, stirring regularly, or until the onion is softened and lightly browned.

2. Stir in the chipotle paste and cook for 1 minute more.

3. Add the chopped tomatoes and beans, then refill a can with water and tip it into the pan. Crumble over the stock cube and bring to a simmer, stirring occasionally. Cook for 15 minutes, stirring regularly.

4. Season to taste then spoon the chicken and beans into four deep bowls and divide the yoghurt between them. Serve with cauli-rice (see page 208), a large portion of cooked green vegetables, and sprinkle over the fresh coriander.

COOK'S TIP

If you don't have chipotle paste, use 2 tablespoons tomato purée mixed with 1–2 teaspoons hot smoked paprika instead.

PER SERVING | **377cals** | PROTEIN **40g** | CARBS **24.4g** | FAT **12.1g** | FIBRE **4.9g**

Chicken dhansak-ish

SERVES 4 | **PREP** 15 mins | **COOK** 40 mins

2 tbsp coconut or canola oil
1 large onion, peeled and finely chopped
6 boneless, skinless chicken thighs (around 600g total weight), trimmed of fat and quartered
3 garlic cloves, peeled and finely grated
25g fresh root ginger, peeled and finely grated
2 tbsp medium Indian curry paste, such as tikka masala or rogan josh
1 × 400g can chopped tomatoes
1 chicken stock cube
100g dried red split lentils
small handful freshly chopped coriander leaves
lime wedges, to serve

COOK'S TIP

If you don't have any curry paste, use 1½ tablespoons curry powder, or a mix of spices, such as a teaspoon each of ground cumin, ground coriander, ground turmeric and chilli powder.

Forget the myth that curries are unhealthy – we are big fans, so long as they are not accompanied by white rice, chapattis and potatoes! You can enjoy this lovely chicken, tomato and lentil curry guilt free.

1. Heat the oil in a large wide-based saucepan or flameproof casserole, add the onion and chicken and fry over a medium-high heat for 10 minutes, until the onion is well softened and beginning to brown, stirring regularly.

2. Add the garlic, ginger and curry paste and cook for 1 minute more, stirring constantly.

3. Tip the chopped tomatoes into the pan with 600ml water. Crumble in the stock cube and stir in the lentils. Season with salt and ground black pepper and bring to a simmer. Cover the pan loosely with a lid, reduce the heat and simmer gently for 30 minutes, until the chicken is tender and the lentils well softened. Stir regularly, especially towards the end of the cooking time.

4. Scatter the coriander over the top and serve with lime wedges, cauli-rice (see page 208) and plenty of finely sliced steamed cabbage. Top each serving with a tablespoon of full-fat live Greek yoghurt, if you like, for an extra 20cals.

Creamy chicken and mushrooms

SERVES
2

PREP
5
mins

COOK
12
mins

4 tsp olive or canola oil

300g chicken breast
  mini fillets

150g chestnut (or button)
  mushrooms, sliced or
  quartered, depending on size

2 spring onions, trimmed
  and finely sliced

200ml chicken stock
  (made with ½ stock cube)

4 tbsp full-fat crème fraîche
  (around 50g)

A glorious one-pan dish, similar to one that my grandmother used to make. Fermented dairy, such as crème fraîche, adds protein, important nutrients, including calcium and iodine, and natural fat that keeps you feeling full for longer.

1. Heat 2 teaspoons of the oil in a large, deep, non-stick frying pan. Season the chicken with ground black pepper and fry over medium-high heat for 2 minutes on each side, or until lightly browned. Transfer to a plate.

2. Add the remaining oil to the pan and fry the mushrooms for 2 minutes, or until lightly browned. Add the spring onions and cook for 30 seconds more, stirring.

3. Return the chicken to the pan, add the stock and bring to the boil. Reduce the heat and simmer for 5 minutes, or until the liquid is reduced to around 4 tablespoons and the chicken is cooked through, stirring occasionally.

4. Stir in the crème fraîche and simmer for 20–30 seconds.

5. Adjust the seasoning to taste and serve with lots of freshly cooked green vegetables.

Cardamom chicken

SERVES
4

PREP
15
mins

COOK
30
mins

2 tbsp olive, coconut
   or canola oil
1 large onion, peeled
   and finely chopped
2 large red capsicums,
   deseeded and cut into
   roughly 2cm chunks
8 cardamom pods,
   lightly crushed
5–6 boneless, skinless chicken
   thighs (around 550g total
   weight), trimmed of fat
   and quartered
20g fresh root ginger,
   peeled and finely chopped
1 tsp cumin seeds
½ tsp crushed dried
   chilli flakes
1 tsp garam masala
400ml chicken stock
   (made with 1 stock cube)
4 tbsp full-fat crème fraîche or
   double cream (around 50g)
small handful fresh coriander
   leaves, to serve

This is a gorgeous, creamy dish, delicately spiced
and flavoured with cardamom.

1. Heat the oil in a large frying pan, add the onion,
capsicums and cardamom and fry over a fairly high heat for
5–6 minutes, or until the onions are browning, stirring
occasionally.

2. Add the chicken and ginger and cook for a further
3 minutes, stirring. Sprinkle over the cumin, chilli
and garam masala and fry for 30 seconds more, stirring.

3. Pour over the stock, season well and bring to a gentle
simmer. Cook for 20 minutes, or until the chicken is tender
and the sauce is well reduced, stirring occasionally.

4. Add the crème fraîche and cook for a final 1–2
minutes, stirring.

5. Serve topped with lots of coriander, roasted cauliflower
(see page 209) and large portions of cooked green
vegetables. (Try to avoid eating the cardamom pods.)

PER SERVING | **318cals** | PROTEIN **40g** | CARBS **6g** | FAT **14.5g** | FIBRE **1.5g**

Chicken katsu curry

SERVES **4** | PREP **15** mins | COOK **25** mins

4 boneless, skinless
chicken breast fillets
(each around 150g)
1 tbsp coconut oil, melted,
or olive or canola oil
50g flaked almonds

For the sauce
1 tbsp olive, coconut
or canola oil
1 medium onion, peeled
and roughly chopped
1 garlic clove, peeled and
finely chopped
15g fresh root ginger,
peeled and finely chopped
1 tsp medium curry powder
¼ tsp Chinese five
spice powder
4 soft dried apricots,
roughly chopped
300ml chicken stock
(made with ½ cube)

This nutty, katsu-style curry is nicely low-carb.
We top it with flaked almonds instead of breadcrumbs
and serve it with a simple sauce flavoured with five
spice and sweetened with apricots.

1. Preheat the oven to 200°C/fan 180°C/Gas 6 and line
a large baking tray with non-stick baking paper.

2. Place the chicken breasts on the tray and brush with a
little oil. Season with salt and ground black pepper. Sprinkle
the almonds on to the chicken, covering as best as you can,
but don't worry if a few nuts fall off. Bake for 20–25 minutes,
or until cooked through and the almonds are lightly toasted.

3. Meanwhile, to make the sauce, heat the oil in a
small saucepan, add the onion, garlic and ginger, and
fry over a low heat for 6–8 minutes, or until softened,
stirring regularly.

4. Add the curry powder and five spice and cook for a few
seconds more, stirring. Stir in the apricots and stock and
bring to a simmer. Cook for 5 minutes, or until the apricots
are softened, stirring regularly.

5. Remove the pan from the heat and blitz the sauce with
a stick blender, or let it cool slightly and blitz in a food
processor, until very smooth. Season to taste.

6. Serve the chicken and any toasted almonds left on
the baking tray with the sauce and a large green salad
or steamed greens.

PER SERVING | **426cals** | PROTEIN **57g** | CARBS **23g** | FAT **11g** | FIBRE **5.5g**

Fastest spaghetti Bolognese

SERVES **4** | **PREP** **15** mins | **COOK** **23** mins

A brilliantly versatile and quick-to-prepare Bolognese. Made with turkey, rather than beef mince, it can be adapted for all sorts of dishes and freezes well.

2 tbsp olive oil
1 medium onion, peeled and finely chopped
500g turkey breast mince
200g small mushrooms, quartered
1 × 400g can chopped tomatoes
2 tbsp tomato purée
1 chicken stock cube
1 tsp dried oregano
20g Parmesan, finely grated

For the spaghetti
80g wholewheat spaghetti
2 large zucchinis, trimmed and spiralized or peeled into ribbons, or use a pack of zoodles

1. Heat the oil in a large non-stick frying or sauté pan, add the onion and mushrooms and fry over a medium-high heat for 5 minutes, stirring regularly.

2. Add the turkey and fry for a further 5–8 minutes, or until lightly browned.

3. Meanwhile, cook the spaghetti in a large pan of boiling water for 10–12 minutes, or according to the pack instructions.

4. Tip the tomatoes into the pan with the mince, stir in 400ml water, the tomato purée, crumbled stock cube and oregano. Bring to a simmer and cook for 5–10 minutes, stirring regularly, until thick. Season with salt and ground black pepper.

5. Add the zucchini to the pan with the pasta and cook for 30 seconds more. Drain in a colander and divide between four warmed bowls or deep plates. Top with the Bolognese, sprinkle with the Parmesan and serve with a green salad or finely sliced steamed greens.

COOK'S TIP

This Bolognese makes a great stuffing for capsicums. On a non-fast day, mix it with cooked lentils and top with grated mozzarella.

Turkey keema

SERVES **4** | **PREP** **10** mins | **COOK** **20** mins

2 tbsp olive, coconut
   or canola oil
1 medium onion, peeled
   and finely chopped
500g turkey breast mince
3 tbsp medium Indian curry
   paste, such as rogan josh
   or tikka masala
1 × 400g can chopped tomatoes
1 chicken stock cube
2 large eggs
small handful freshly
   chopped coriander,
   to serve (optional)

Keema is a traditional Indian mince and pea curry, and is super with a dollop of full-fat live Greek yoghurt, mixed with grated cucumber and a pinch of cumin seeds. On a non-fast day, serve with a Wholemeal mini flatbread (see page 236).

1. Heat the oil in a large, deep, non-stick frying pan, add the onion and turkey and fry for 8–10 minutes over a medium-high heat, or until lightly browned, stirring regularly and breaking up the mince.

2. Add the curry paste and cook for 1 minute, stirring constantly. Add the tomatoes, crumbled stock cube and 300ml water. Bring to a simmer and cook for about 10 minutes, stirring regularly, until thick. Season with salt and ground black pepper.

3. Meanwhile, half fill a medium saucepan with water and bring to the boil. Gently add the eggs, return to the boil and cook for 8 minutes.

4. Rinse the eggs under cold running water until cool enough to handle, then peel and cut them into quarters. Place on top of the keema, scatter over the coriander, if using, and serve with cauli-rice (see page 208) and a colourful salad. Or simply serve on a base of finely sliced cooked cabbage.

Five spice duck with chilli and plum sauce

SERVES | PREP | COOK
2 | **5** mins | **20** mins

½ tsp Chinese five
  spice powder
2 duck breast portions
  (each around 125g),
  skin lightly scored
½ tsp crushed dried
  chilli flakes, to taste
320–350g ready-prepared
  stir-fry vegetables
2 tbsp plum or hoisin sauce,
  from a bottle or jar

COOK'S TIP

After roasting for 15 minutes, the duck should be cooked through but slightly pink in the middle. If you prefer your duck more pink, roast for about 12 minutes instead.

This simple, Chinese-inspired dish makes a filling, high-protein supper and is a great way to start if you have never cooked duck before.

1. Preheat the oven to 200°C/fan 180°C/Gas 6 and line a small roasting tin with foil.

2. Mix the five spice powder with a generous pinch each of flaked sea salt and ground black pepper in a small bowl. Season the underside of the duck (not the skin) with this five-spice mixture.

3. Place a large frying pan over a medium heat and, when hot, add the breasts, skin side down. Cook for 5 minutes, or until the skin is nicely browned, then turn and cook on the other side for 1 minute. Transfer the duck to the roasting tin, skin side up, and spoon out all but around 1 tablespoon of the duck fat from the frying pan. Keep the pan aside to cook the vegetables.

4. Roast the duck for 15 minutes, sprinkling the crushed dried chilli over the top for the last 5 minutes. Transfer to a board, cover loosely with foil and leave to rest for 5 minutes.

5. Meanwhile, return the pan to a high heat and stir-fry the vegetables for 3–4 minutes, in the remaining duck fat, until tender-crisp. Add the plum or hoisin sauce and toss with the vegetables for 20–30 seconds, or until hot.

6. Divide the veg between two warmed plates, slice the duck breasts and place on top. Serve with half a plate of steamed pak choi or other cooked greens.

Beef, Pork and Lamb

While we are advised to reduce the amount of red meat we eat, beef, pork and lamb provide highly nutritious sources of protein and nutrients, like iron, on a fasting day. A little goes a long way. Choose better quality, while eating less.

PER SERVING | **358cals** | PROTEIN **47.5g** | CARBS **5.5g** | FAT **14.5g** | FIBRE **8g**

Steak and chips

SERVES **4** | **PREP** **15** mins | **COOK** **35** mins

2 large tomatoes, halved
4 × 200g beef steaks,
    such as rump or sirloin
2 tsp coarsely ground
    black pepper
1 tbsp olive or canola oil
3 large flat or Portobello
    mushrooms, sliced

For the celeriac chips
750g celeriac, peeled and cut
    into 1–1.5cm-thick 'chips'
    (around 575g peeled weight)
1 tbsp olive or canola oil

COOK'S TIP

Cut off and discard
any fat before eating.

Yes, you can have steak and chips on the Fast 800!
Only here, the chips are made from celeriac, to keep
the starchy carbs low.

1. Preheat the oven to 220°C/fan 200°C/Gas 7.

2. Place the celeriac chips in a bowl, add the oil, a couple
of pinches of flaked sea salt and lots of ground black pepper,
and toss them well together. Scatter over a large baking
tray and bake for 20 minutes.

3. Remove the chips from the oven and turn them. Place
the tomatoes on the same tray, cut side up, season and bake
for a further 15 minutes, or until the tomatoes are softened.

4. Meanwhile, season the steaks on both sides with a little
flaked sea salt and the ground black pepper. Heat the oil in
a large frying pan over a medium-high heat, add the steaks
and fry for about 3 minutes on each side for medium-rare,
depending on thickness. Divide the steaks between 4
warmed plates and leave to rest for 4–5 minutes.

5. Meanwhile, return the pan to the heat, add the sliced
mushrooms and fry for 2–3 minutes, or until lightly
browned, turning regularly.

6. Serve the steak, mushrooms, chips and tomatoes
with a generous green side salad or cooked leafy greens.

Spicy beef 'tacos'

SERVES **2**

PREP **10** mins

COOK **8** mins

250g lean minced beef
(around 10% fat)
1 capsicum, any colour,
deseeded and cut into
1.5cm chunks
1 small onion, peeled and
finely chopped
½ tsp ground cumin
1 tsp ground coriander
¼ tsp hot chilli powder or
crushed dried chilli flakes
2 tbsp tomato purée
15g bunch fresh coriander,
leaves finely chopped,
plus extra to serve
2 Little Gem lettuces, trimmed
and leaves separated
100g full-fat live Greek
yoghurt
lime or lemon wedges,
to serve

A classic Tex-Mex dish that is still on the menu thanks to the lettuce 'tacos'. On a non-fast day, you can serve them with grated Cheddar, sliced avocado and full-fat soured cream, instead of the yoghurt.

1. Place a large, non-stick frying pan over a medium–high heat, add the minced beef, capsicum and chopped onion and fry for 5 minutes, or until the beef is cooked through, stirring and breaking up the meat.

2. Sprinkle over the spices, season with a pinch of salt and lots of ground black pepper and cook for 1 minute. Add the tomato purée and cook another minute, stirring constantly.

3. Stir in 6 tablespoons cold water, sizzle for a few more seconds, then remove the pan from the heat and fold through the coriander.

4. Divide the lettuce leaves between two plates and fill the leaves with the mince. Top with the yoghurt and remaining coriander and serve with a squeeze of lime or lemon.

PER SERVING | **294cals** | PROTEIN **30.5g** | CARBS **14.5g** | FAT **12g** | FIBRE **5g**

Beef and black bean stir-fry

SERVES **2** | PREP **10** mins | COOK **8** mins

250g beef frying steak, trimmed of fat and cut into 1.5cm thin strips
1 tbsp olive or canola oil
1 medium onion, peeled and cut into thin wedges
2 small capsicums, any colour, deseeded and cut into 1–1.5cm slices
1 garlic clove, peeled and finely chopped
10g fresh root ginger, peeled and cut into thin matchsticks
3 tbsp black bean stir-fry sauce, from a jar or sachet (around 40g)
1 red chilli, finely sliced, or 1 tsp crushed dried chilli flakes, to serve (optional)

COOK'S TIP

Frying steak from the supermarket is less expensive than a premium cut, but you could use sirloin or rump steak instead.

Michael and I always choose this at our brilliant local Chinese restaurant, but now we can also make it at home. Black bean sauce is made from fermented soya beans, which give the sauce its characteristic tangy flavour.

1. Season the beef well with a little salt and lots of ground black pepper.

2. Heat 2 teaspoons of the oil in a large frying pan or wok over a high heat. Add the beef and stir-fry for 1 minute, or until lightly browned but not cooked through. Transfer the beef to a plate.

3. Return the pan to the heat, add the remaining oil, onion and capsicums, and stir-fry for 4 minutes, or until just softened.

4. Add the garlic and ginger and cook for 1 minute more.

5. Pour over the black bean sauce, then return the beef to the pan. Add 4 tablespoons cold water and cook for 1–2 minutes, or until the beef is hot and glossy, stirring regularly.

6. Scatter the chilli over the top, if using, and serve with cauli-rice (see page 208), steamed sliced cabbage or zoodles (see page 120).

Simple beef casserole

SERVES **4** | **PREP** **15** mins | **COOK** **140** mins

600g braising or stewing steak,
   cut into 3–4cm chunks
1 tbsp olive or canola oil
1 medium onion, peeled
   and roughly chopped
3 celery sticks, trimmed
   and cut into 2cm slices
2 large carrots (around 300g
   total weight), well washed,
   trimmed, halved lengthways
   and cut into 2cm slices
1 × 400g can chopped tomatoes
1 tsp dried mixed herbs
1 beef stock cube

COOK'S TIP

Try and choose beef with
a little fat marbling. Lean
beef that has been heavily
trimmed won't be nearly
as tender.

A really easy and comforting stew that takes very
little time to prepare and can be left bubbling away
in the oven while you do other things.

1. Preheat the oven to 180°C/fan 160°C/Gas 4.
Season the beef all over with a little salt and lots
of ground black pepper.

2. Heat the oil in a medium flameproof casserole,
add the beef and onion and fry over a medium-high
heat for 5 minutes, or until the onion is softened
and beginning to brown.

3. Add the celery, carrots, tomatoes and mixed herbs.
Fill the empty tomato can with water and tip this into
the pan (you'll need around 400ml water). Crumble
over the stock cube and stir well. Bring to a simmer,
then cover with a lid and cook in the oven for
2–2¼ hours, or until the beef is very tender.

4. Remove from the oven and serve with lots of
green veg – shredded Savoy cabbage or kale goes
particularly well.

Lamb and chickpea curry

SERVES | PREP | COOK
4 | **10** mins | **105** mins

1 tbsp coconut or canola oil
1 medium onion, peeled and
   thinly sliced
500g lamb neck fillets,
   trimmed of fat and cut
   into roughly 3cm chunks
1 tsp red chilli paste from a
   jar or tube, or 1 red chilli,
   finely chopped
1 tsp ginger paste from a jar or
   tube, or 1 tsp finely grated
   fresh root ginger
4 tbsp medium Indian curry
   paste (around 60g), such as
   rogan josh or tikka masala
1 × 400g can chopped tomatoes
1 × 400g can chickpeas in water
200g spinach leaves, tough
   stalks removed
3 tbsp full-fat live Greek
   yoghurt, plus extra to serve

COOK'S TIP

If you buy chickpeas
without additives, you
can add them with the
liquid from the can.
If they contain firming
agents, drain first and
add 100ml water instead.

A handy and satisfying curry that makes the most of store-cupboard ingredients. This is filling enough to serve as it is, but on non-fast days, you can add a small portion of brown rice or a Wholemeal mini flatbread (see page 236).

1. Preheat the oven to 180°C/fan 160°C/Gas 4.

2. Heat the oil in a medium flameproof casserole, add the onion and cook over a moderate heat for 3 minutes, stirring regularly.

3. Add the lamb, season with salt and ground black pepper and cook for 3–4 minutes, or until lightly coloured on all sides, stirring regularly. Add the chilli, ginger and curry paste and cook for 2 minutes, stirring.

4. Tip the tomatoes and chickpeas with their liquid (see tip below) into the casserole, half fill the tomato can with water and stir that in. Bring to a simmer and cover with a lid. Transfer to the oven and cook for about 1½ hours or until the lamb is very tender.

5. Remove from the oven and stir in the spinach and yoghurt. (If using large spinach leaves, you may need to return the pan to the oven for 5–10 minutes, but young spinach won't need any additional cooking.) Adjust the seasoning to taste and serve with more yoghurt, if you like, but don't forget to add the calories. Feel free to add a salad or extra cooked greens.

Lamb burgers

SERVES **4**

PREP **10** mins

COOK **10** mins

500g minced lamb
  (20% fat or less)
6 spring onions, trimmed
  and very finely sliced
1 garlic clove, peeled
  and finely grated
1 medium zucchini
  (around 175g), trimmed
  and finely grated
½ tsp dried mint
½ tsp flaked sea salt

COOK'S TIP

For a little extra spice, add ¼ teaspoon ground cinnamon to the burger mix.

These lamb burgers couldn't be simpler and make a great alternative to beef.

1. Place all the ingredients in a bowl, season with lots of ground black pepper and combine thoroughly with your hands.

2. Divide the mixture into 4 balls and flatten into burgers, each around 12cm wide. Make them a little flatter than you think they should be, as they will shrink as they cook.

3. Place a large non-stick frying pan over a medium heat, add the burgers and cook for about 10 minutes, or until lightly browned and cooked through, turning once or twice. Press the burgers every now and then with a spatula so they cook evenly.

4. Serve with a large mixed salad and some tzatziki (see page 91) for an extra 61cals per portion.

Individual moussakas

SERVES **4** | **PREP** **10** mins | **COOK** **40** mins

2 medium eggplants
  (each around 240g)
2 tsp olive oil
400g lamb mince,
  around 20% fat
1 medium onion, peeled
  and finely chopped
2 garlic cloves, peeled
  and crushed
1 tsp dried oregano
½ tsp dried mint
1 × 400g can chopped tomatoes
1 lamb or beef stock cube
1 tbsp tomato purée
150g feta

COOK'S TIP

The moussakas can be frozen for up to 1 month, after topping with feta but before roasting. Defrost thoroughly then reheat in the oven at 200°C/fan 180°C/Gas 6 for 20–25 minutes, or until hot throughout.

Eggplants, with their delicious silky flesh, contain lots of antioxidants and are said to reduce blood sugars and aid weight loss. This is an easy and delicious way to enjoy them.

1. Preheat the oven to 200°C/fan 180°C/Gas 6.

2. Cut the eggplants in half lengthways and score the flesh in a criss-cross pattern without cutting all the way through to the skin. Place the eggplants halves in a shallow ovenproof dish, cut side up, and brush with the oil. Bake for 30–35 minutes, or until softened and lightly browned.

3. Meanwhile, place the mince in a large non-stick frying pan with the onion and fry over a medium heat for 6–8 minutes, or until onion has softened, stirring and breaking up the meat. Sprinkle over the garlic, oregano and mint and cook for a few seconds more.

4. Add the tomatoes, crumbled stock cube and tomato purée and bring to a simmer. Cook for 5 minutes, stirring regularly. Season to taste.

5. Remove the eggplants from the oven and spoon the mince mixture on top. Crumble the feta over the mince and return to the oven for 10 minutes, or until the feta is softened and lightly browned.

6. Remove from the oven and serve with a large green salad.

Lamb hot pot

SERVES	PREP	COOK
4	**10** mins	**120** mins

500g lamb neck fillets,
    trimmed of fat and cut
    into roughly 3cm chunks
1 medium onion, peeled
    and sliced
4 medium carrots (around
    350g total weight), well
    washed, trimmed and cut
    into roughly 2cm slices
700ml lamb stock
    (made with 1 cube)
50g pearl barley
1 tsp dried mint
1 tbsp Worcestershire sauce
100g frozen peas

Based on a Pattison family favourite, this recipe skips out the browning stage, so all you need do is combine the ingredients in a casserole and leave them to simmer slowly in the oven.

1. Preheat the oven to 180°C/ fan 160°C/Gas 4.

2. Place all the ingredients in a medium casserole and season with a little salt and lots of ground black pepper. Stir well, cover and cook in the oven for about 2 hours, or until the lamb is very tender and the pearl barley is soft.

3. Remove from the oven, stir in the peas and return to the oven for a further 5–10 minutes.

4. Remove from the oven, adjust the seasoning to taste and serve with large portions of freshly cooked green vegetables.

COOK'S TIP

Some lamb neck fillet can be quite fatty. There is no need to remove all the fat, just the particularly hard bits that are easy to reach.

Puy lentils with mushrooms and sausages

SERVES
2

PREP
10
mins

COOK
15
mins

2 tsp olive oil
4 good-quality chipolata
  sausages
1 medium onion, peeled
  and thinly sliced
200g chestnut (or button)
  mushrooms, sliced or
  quartered, depending on size
100g cherry tomatoes, halved
1 garlic clove, peeled
  and crushed
½ tsp dried thyme
125g cooked puy lentils
  (half a pre-cooked pouch
  or from a can)
1 tbsp cider vinegar

COOK'S TIP

We use half a 250g pouch
pre-cooked puy lentils,
but you could use dried
lentils instead. You will
need around 65g dried
lentils to give around
125g when cooked.
Add ½ vegetable stock
cube to the water when
boiling, for extra flavour.

Deliciously filling comfort food – and ready in under 15 minutes. The lentils are a great source of extra nutrients and fibre. You can swap the sausages in this recipe for other protein sources, such as halloumi, cooked chicken or ham (see page 239).

1. Heat the oil in a large frying pan, add the sausages and fry for 5–6 minutes over a medium-high heat, turning regularly until lightly browned on all sides and just cooked. Transfer to a plate.

2. Reduce the heat to medium, add the onion and mushrooms and fry for 5 minutes, or until lightly browned, stirring regularly.

3. Stir in the tomatoes, garlic and thyme and cook for 1 minute, stirring.

4. Return the sausages to the pan, add the lentils and 150ml water and cook for 2–3 minutes, stirring regularly, until the lentils and sausages are hot throughout and the tomatoes are softened but not falling apart.

5. Season with the vinegar and some salt and ground black pepper to taste. Bubble for 20–30 seconds and serve with plenty of steamed leafy greens.

Stir-fried pork with green beans

SERVES
2

PREP
5
mins

COOK
10
mins

1 tbsp canola oil
175g green beans,
    trimmed and halved if large
250g lean minced pork (5% fat)
6 spring onions, trimmed
    and cut into 1cm slices
2 tbsp hoisin sauce
1 red chilli, finely sliced,
    to serve (optional)

COOK'S TIP

If you don't have any
hoisin sauce, try plum,
teriyaki or oyster sauce
instead. The calories will
vary a little. Without the
hoisin sauce, the recipe
contains 248cals and
28g protein per serving.

A brilliantly simple and speedy lunch or supper
dish. If you aren't keen on pork, use minced turkey
or chicken instead.

1. Heat the oil in a large frying pan or wok, add the
beans and stir-fry over a high heat for 2 minutes,
or until beginning to soften, stirring regularly.

2. Add the pork and cook for 4 minutes, breaking up the
mince as it cooks, or until the beans are lightly toasted
in places and the pork is browning.

3. Scatter over the spring onions and cook for 1 minute
more, stirring.

4. Spoon the hoisin sauce and 5 tablespoons water into the
pan, and cook for 2 minutes, or until the sauce looks rich
and glossy and lightly coats the pork, stirring constantly.

5. Sprinkle with chilli, if using, and serve as a quick lunch
with ribbons of cooked cabbage or leafy greens. Or make
more of a meal with cauli-rice (see page 208) or a side
of stir-fried veg (see page 198).

PER SERVING | **379cals** | PROTEIN **16g** | CARBS **10g** | FAT **30g** | FIBRE **3g**

Low-carb sausage 'lasagne'

SERVES **6** | PREP **15** mins | COOK **40** mins

6 good-quality sausages
  (around 400g total weight)
2 medium onions, peeled
  and finely chopped
2 garlic cloves, peeled
  and finely chopped
1 tsp dried oregano
1 × 400g can chopped tomatoes
250g young spinach leaves
2 medium zucchinis, trimmed
  and sliced lengthways into
  strips 3–4mm thick
good pinch ground nutmeg
200g full-fat crème fraîche
40g Parmesan, finely grated

COOK'S TIP

Avoid cooking this dish for any longer than stated, as the zucchinis will release more liquid as they bake.

This easy low-carb 'lasagne' was created during a brilliant Zoom session when we had to come up with a dish using specific ingredients. These included sausages, tinned tomatoes and spinach. We skipped the starchy lasagne sheets and used layers of zucchini instead.

1. Preheat the oven to 200°C/fan 180°C/Gas 6.

2. Place a shallow, flameproof casserole over a medium heat. Squeeze the sausages out of their skins and into the pan in small chunks. Add the onions and fry together, stirring, for 10 minutes, or until the onion is softened and the sausages are lightly browned. Add the garlic and oregano and cook for a few seconds. Tip the tomatoes into the pan and simmer for 5 minutes, stirring regularly, until thick.

3. Place the spinach in a colander in the sink and pour just-boiled water over the top until it softens. Otherwise, you can soften it in the microwave. Leave to stand until cool enough to handle, then squeeze the leaves to remove as much water as possible.

4. Remove the casserole from the heat and season well. Place the zucchini slices over the sausage mixture, then top with the spinach leaves.

5. Stir the nutmeg into the crème fraîche and spread over the spinach – you don't need to be too neat. Sprinkle with the Parmesan and season with more ground black pepper. Bake for 20–25 minutes, or until starting to brown.

6. Remove from the oven and serve with a large green salad.

PER SERVING | **288cals** | PROTEIN **34g** | CARBS **1g** | FAT **16g** | FIBRE **1g**

Pork with mustard and cider vinegar

SERVES **2** | **PREP** **5** mins | **COOK** **10** mins

1 tbsp olive oil

300g pork medallions, or tenderloin fillet, trimmed of fat and cut into 6 slices

2 tsp wholegrain mustard

2 tbsp full-fat crème fraîche (around 25g)

1 tbsp cider vinegar

10g bunch fresh parsley, leaves finely chopped

COOK'S TIP

If you don't like pork, you could use sliced, skinless chicken breast fillets (around 150g) instead. Made with chicken, this dish will have 267cals and 37g protein per serving.

This family favourite proved a hit on our Channel 4 series 'Lose a Stone in 21 Days' and on Instagram, too, where we cooked it with pork steaks, rather than tenderloin. It's simple and luxurious.

1. Heat the oil in a small non-stick frying pan over a moderate heat. Season the pork and cook for 3–4 minutes, or until starting to brown. Turn and fry on the other side for a further 3–4 minutes, or until just cooked through.

2. Meanwhile, mix together the mustard, crème fraîche and vinegar in a small bowl. Add half the parsley, a pinch of salt and a generous amount of freshly ground black pepper.

3. Reduce the heat and pour over the mustard sauce over the pork. Stir to incorporate any cooking juices. Add a splash of water and simmer for 1–2 minutes, or until sauce is hot, stirring.

4. Remove from the heat, scatter the remaining parsley over the top and serve with mounds of freshly cooked green veg.

Meat Free

A vegetarian diet is wonderfully high in fibre, which is great for your microbiome. However, on an 800cals day, getting enough protein can be a challenge, so we have included a lot of tips and swaps to enable you to boost your intake. You can also check the Toolkit on page 239.

PER SERVING | **339cals** | PROTEIN **21.5g** | CARBS **24g** | FAT **16g** | FIBRE **7.5g**

Tofu mushroom ramen

SERVES **2** | PREP **15** mins | COOK **10** mins

10g dried mushrooms,
   mixed or porcini
2 tbsp red miso paste,
   or any other miso
2 tsp olive or canola oil
150g extra-firm tofu,
   cut into 4 slices
25g plain cashews,
   very roughly chopped
40g dried wholewheat noodles
125g closed cup or shiitake
   mushrooms, sliced
1 pak choi, trimmed and
   thickly sliced, leaving
   any smaller leaves whole
100g beansprouts, rinsed
   and drained
4 spring onions, trimmed
   and very finely sliced
crushed dried chilli flakes
   or freshly sliced red chilli,
   to serve (optional)

COOK'S TIP

If you can't find firm tofu,
use silken tofu instead but
don't fry it. Instead, cut into
cubes and warm through
in the stock for a couple
of minutes before serving.

Tofu is a great source of protein and helps make
this dish deliciously satisfying. Add finely sliced fresh
root ginger and garlic to the broth for extra flavour,
and season with a splash of soy sauce.

1. Place the dried mushrooms in a large wide-based
saucepan and add 1 litre of just-boiled water. Stir in
the miso paste to make a broth and leave to stand for
15 minutes.

2. Meanwhile, heat the oil in a large non-stick frying
pan, add the tofu slices and fry over a medium heat for
2½ minutes, or until lightly browned. Turn the tofu, add
the nuts and fry for a further 2½ minutes, stirring regularly.

3. Add the noodles, closed cup or shiitake mushrooms
and pak choi to the saucepan with the dried mushrooms
and miso. Bring to a simmer and cook for 3 minutes,
stirring to separate the noodles.

4. Stir in the beansprouts and spring onions and cook
for 1 minute.

5. Divide the noodles, mushrooms and vegetables
between two deep, wide bowls and top with the tofu.
Ladle over the broth and sprinkle with the chopped
nuts and chilli, if using.

Roasted veg with cumin and goat's cheese

SERVES	PREP	COOK
4	**15** mins	**30** mins

3 capsicums, any colour,
   deseeded and cut into
   3cm chunks
2 large zucchinis, trimmed,
   halved lengthways and
   cut into 2cm chunks
1 red onion, peeled and cut
   into thin wedges
2 tbsp extra-virgin olive oil
1 tsp ground cumin
20 cherry tomatoes
   (around 200g)
50g mixed seeds
200g soft goat's cheese,
   or any soft cheese
handful rocket leaves
lemon wedges, to serve

Rich in Mediterranean goodness, the sweet, roasted veg here is flavoured with bursts of salty, goat's cheese. On a non-fast day, you could serve this with a few tablespoons of cooked lentils, quinoa, a thin slice of wholegrain bread or a Wholemeal mini flatbread (see page 236).

1. Preheat the oven to 200°C/fan 180°C/Gas 6.

2. Place all the vegetables together in a bowl and toss with 1 tablespoon of the oil, the cumin, a generous pinch of flaked sea salt and lots of ground black pepper. Scatter over a large baking tray and roast for 20 minutes.

3. Remove from the oven, add the tomatoes and sprinkle with the seeds. Cook for a further 10 minutes, or until all the vegetables are tender and lightly browned.

4. Break the cheese into chunky pieces and place on top of the veg. Scatter over the rocket, drizzle with the remaining oil and add a squeeze of lemon before serving.

PER SERVING | **421cals** | PROTEIN **21.3g** | CARBS **28.2g** | FAT **22.3g** | FIBRE **11.3g**

One pan miso eggplant with peanuts

SERVES **2** | PREP **10** mins | COOK **40** mins

2 medium eggplants
2 tsp extra-virgin olive oil
2 tbsp miso paste
1 tbsp dark soy sauce
20g fresh root ginger,
    peeled and finely grated
½ tsp crushed dried
    chilli flakes
50g plain peanuts or
    cashews, roughly chopped
2 spring onions, trimmed
    and finely sliced
100g frozen edamame
1 red chilli, finely sliced,
    to serve

COOK'S TIP

If you don't have any
fresh ginger, use 1 tablespoon
ginger purée or 1 teaspoon
ground ginger instead.

Miso paste brings a sweet, exotic and slightly salty flavour to the eggplant. This makes a filling supper for two or can be shared between four. It is delicious with a Chinese leaf salad or steamed broccoli.

1. Preheat the oven to 200°C/fan 180°C/Gas 6 and line a baking tray with foil.

2. Cut the eggplants in half lengthways and score the flesh in a criss-cross pattern, without cutting all the way through to the skin. Place on the baking tray, cut side up, and brush with the oil. Bake for about 30 minutes, or until softened and lightly browned.

3. Meanwhile, mix the miso paste with the soy sauce, ginger and chilli flakes in a small bowl. In a separate bowl, combine the peanuts and spring onions.

4. Remove the baking tray from the oven and spread the eggplants with the miso mixture. Sprinkle the spring onions and peanuts over the top and scatter the frozen edamame on to the tray around the eggplants. Return to the oven for a further 8–10 minutes, or until the peanuts are lightly browned and the edamame are hot.

5. Scatter over the chilli to serve. You can scoop the roasted eggplant out of the skins as you eat – even better, eat the skins, too.

| PER SERVING | **382cals** | PROTEIN **17g** | CARBS **22g** | FAT **21.5g** | FIBRE **7g**

Mushroom and cashew Bourguignon

SERVES | PREP | COOK
4 | **10** mins | **25** mins

15g dried mushrooms,
    porcini or mixed
2 tbsp olive or canola oil
1 medium onion, peeled
    and finely chopped
500g chestnut (or button)
    mushrooms, halved or
    quartered if large
100g dried green lentils
120g plain cashews or other
    nuts, roughly chopped
100ml red wine or water
1 vegetable stock cube
2 tbsp tomato purée
1 tsp dried mixed herbs

COOK'S TIP

When you add the soaked
mushrooms and their liquor
in step 3, take care to avoid
including any deposits that
may have settled at the
bottom of the jug.

I love mushrooms and would encourage eating lots, as
they have amazing antioxidant properties, protecting
against heart disease and cancer, as well as containing
beta glucans known to help regulate blood sugars.

1. Place the dried mushrooms in a measuring jug and
cover with 600ml just-boiled water. Stir and leave to
stand for 10 minutes.

2. Heat the oil in a medium flameproof casserole or
wide-based saucepan, add the onion and mushrooms
and fry over a medium heat for 6–8 minutes, or until
the onion is softened and the mushrooms lightly
browned, stirring regularly.

3. Stir in the lentils, soaked mushrooms and their liquor,
the nuts, wine or water, stock cube, tomato purée and
dried herbs. Season with salt and lots of ground black
pepper. Bring to a gentle simmer, cover with a lid and
cook for 20 minutes, stirring occasionally. (The lentils
should be tender but retain their shape.)

4. Serve with lots of freshly cooked green vegetables.

Leek, pea and paneer curry

SERVES
4

PREP
15
mins

COOK
10
mins

2 tbsp canola or coconut oil
2 large leeks, trimmed and
   finely sliced
1 × 225g pack paneer cheese,
   cut into 1.5cm cubes
1 tbsp medium curry powder
2 tsp cumin seeds
15g fresh root ginger,
   peeled and finely chopped,
   or 1 tsp ground ginger
2 large garlic cloves, peeled
   and finely chopped
300g frozen peas
20g fresh coriander,
   leaves roughly chopped,
   plus extra to serve
200g full-fat live Greek
   yoghurt

An easy, tasty, high-protein green curry. Serve with roasted cauliflower (see page 208) and, on a non-fast day, you could have a Wholemeal mini flatbread (see page 236) or a small portion of brown rice and a dollop of full-fat live Greek yoghurt.

1. Heat the oil in a large non-stick frying pan over a medium heat. Add the leeks and paneer and fry gently for 5 minutes, stirring and turning the paneer regularly, until browned on most sides.

2. Add the curry powder, cumin, ginger and garlic. Stir for about 30 seconds, then add the peas and pour over 250ml water. Bring to a simmer and cook for 2–3 minutes, stirring gently, until the peas are hot. Add an extra splash of water, if needed.

3. Stir in the coriander and season to taste with salt and ground black pepper. Divide between four warmed dishes, top with the yoghurt and sprinkle with the remaining coriander to serve.

PER SERVING | **345cals** | PROTEIN **21g** | CARBS **9g** | FAT **23g** | FIBRE **7g**

Curried broccoli with paneer

SERVES | PREP | COOK
3 | **10** mins | **7** mins

1 large head broccoli
(around 450g)
1 tbsp olive or canola oil
200g paneer, cut into
roughly 1.5cm chunks
10 cherry tomatoes, halved
1 garlic clove, peeled and
thinly sliced
½–1 tsp crushed dried
chilli flakes
1 tsp garam masala or
medium curry powder
juice ½ small lemon

Our kids are huge broccoli fans and we're always looking for interesting ways to serve them. This recipe has plenty of flavour and goes nicely with full-fat live Greek yoghurt, but don't forget to add the extra calories (see page 239).

1. Third fill a large saucepan with water and bring to the boil.

2. Meanwhile, place the broccoli on a chopping board and cut off the florets. Cut any large florets in half or into quarters, until they are all roughly the same size. Discard the bottom 2.5cm stalk, then thinly slice the rest into pieces around 5mm thick. Add the broccoli to the pan and return to the boil. Cook for 1 minute, then drain well in a colander.

3. Pour the oil into a large frying pan or wok and place over a medium-high heat. When hot, add the paneer and cook for 1–2 minutes, turning regularly, until lightly browned.

4. Add the broccoli and tomatoes and stir-fry for 2 minutes, then sprinkle the garlic, chilli and garam masala or curry powder over the top and cook for a final 2 minutes, or until the tomatoes have softened, stirring constantly.

5. Season with the lemon juice and lots of ground black pepper to serve.

Indian-inspired chickpea patties

SERVES | **PREP** | **COOK**
4 | **15** mins | **10** mins

2 tbsp coconut or canola oil
1 medium red onion, peeled
    and finely chopped
15g fresh root ginger,
    peeled and finely grated
2 garlic cloves, peeled
    and finely grated
1½ tsp medium curry
    powder or garam masala
1–2 tsp crushed dried chilli
    flakes (optional)
1 × 400g can chickpeas,
    drained
1 tbsp tahini
20g plain peanuts,
    coarsely ground
1 tbsp plain wholemeal flour
15g bunch fresh coriander,
    leaves finely chopped,
    plus extra to serve
1 red chilli, finely sliced,
    to serve
lime wedges, to serve

Enjoy these mildly spiced patties with a lightly dressed green salad and coconut yoghurt (adding the extra calories – see page 239). They are also delicious served cold or as part of a packed lunch.

1. Heat 1 tablespoon of the oil in a medium saucepan over a low-medium heat. Add the onion and fry for 4 minutes, or until beginning to soften, stirring regularly.

2. Add the ginger, garlic, spices and chilli flakes, if using, and cook for 1 minute more, stirring constantly.

3. Remove from the heat, tip the chickpeas into the pan, add the tahini and peanuts, and mash with a potato masher, until the chickpeas turn to a thick paste and clump together (this should take a couple of minutes).

4. Transfer to a bowl, season well with salt and ground black pepper, add the flour and chopped coriander and mix well. Form the mixture into 8 patties, pressing together firmly so they hold their shape.

5. Heat the remaining oil in a large non-stick frying pan over a medium heat. Add the patties and fry for about 5 minutes, or until golden brown and crisp, turning halfway through the cooking time.

6. Serve 2 patties per person with some chilli, if using, a lime wedge, coriander leaves and a large green salad.

COOK'S TIP

To grind the peanuts, use a food processor, spice grinder or stick blender. You can also bash them in a pestle and mortar or very finely chop them on a board.

Creamy cashew and pumpkin curry

SERVES **4** | **PREP** **15** mins | **COOK** **40** mins

1 tbsp olive, coconut
   or canola oil
1 large onion, peeled
   and roughly chopped
100g plain cashews
2 large garlic cloves, peeled
   and finely chopped
3 tbsp medium Indian
   curry paste
300g butternut pumpkin, peeled
   and cut into 2.5cm chunks
3 medium carrots, well
   washed, trimmed and
   cut into 2.5cm chunks
1×400ml can full-fat
   coconut milk
2 capsicums, any colour,
   deseeded and sliced
small handful roughly
   chopped coriander leaves,
   to serve (optional)

A vegetable curry packed with golden vegetables and cashews. Serve with a generous portion of leafy green veg and perhaps some cauli-rice (see page 208). If you like a little more heat, stir in ½–1 teaspoon crushed dried chilli flakes for the last 5 minutes of the cooking time.

1. Heat the oil in a large wide-based saucepan, add the onion and nuts and fry over a medium heat for 5 minutes, or until the onion is softened, stirring regularly.

2. Add the garlic and curry paste and cook for 1 minute, stirring constantly.

3. Add the pumpkin and carrots, pour over the coconut milk and refill the can with water. Pour this water into the pan and stir well. Cover with a lid, bring to a gentle simmer and cook for about 25 minutes, or until the vegetables are almost tender, stirring occasionally.

4. Add the capsicums, return to a simmer and cook, uncovered, for a further 5 minutes, stirring once or twice.

5. Season with salt and ground black pepper and scatter with fresh coriander, if using, to serve.

COOK'S TIP

This curry is a great base for fish or chicken – fry 300g chicken breast chunks with the onions in step 1, or add 300g white fish chunks for the last 5 minutes of the cooking time.

PER SERVING | **397cals** | PROTEIN **12g** | CARBS **19g** | FAT **29g** | FIBRE **4g**

Harissa baked cauliflower with roasted almonds and grapes

SERVES **2** | PREP **10** mins | COOK **30** mins

1 tbsp harissa paste
1 tsp ground cumin
1 tsp ground coriander
2 tbsp olive oil
½ large cauliflower, trimmed and cut into small florets (around 300g prepared weight)
50g flaked almonds
125g seedless red grapes
4 tbsp full-fat live Greek yoghurt (around 50g)
1 small garlic clove, peeled and crushed

COOK'S TIP

Add halloumi for extra protein (see page 239).

Tossing cauliflower in spices before roasting boosts its flavour magnificently. Adding fresh grapes just before the end of the cooking time brings bursts of natural sweetness to this dish. It makes a great light lunch and can also be eaten cold as a packed lunch.

1. Preheat the oven to 200°C/fan 180°C/Gas 6.

2. Mix the harissa, cumin, coriander and oil in a large bowl. Add the cauliflower, season with a generous pinch of salt and lots of ground black pepper and toss well together. Tip on to a large baking tray and roast for 20 minutes.

3. Remove from the oven, scatter the almonds and grapes over the top and roast for a further 10 minutes, or until the almonds are lightly toasted and the grapes softened.

4. Meanwhile, make a dressing by mixing the yoghurt, garlic and 1 tablespoon cold water in a small bowl.

5. Divide the cauliflower, grapes and almonds between two shallow bowls or plates and drizzle with the dressing. Serve with a large green salad.

Quick veggie chilli

1 tbsp olive oil
1 medium onion, peeled
  and finely chopped
350g Quorn mince
1–1½ tsp hot smoked paprika,
  depending on taste
1 tsp ground cumin
1 × 400g can chopped tomatoes
1 × 400g can black beans or
  red kidney beans in water,
  drained and rinsed
1 vegetable stock cube
1 tbsp tomato purée
1 tsp dried oregano or mixed
  dried herbs
small handful fresh coriander
  leaves, to serve (optional)
lime wedges, to serve

COOK'S TIP

You could swap the Quorn
for an extra 400g beans or
lentils. Without the Quorn,
but with extra beans this
recipe contains 209cals and
10.5g protein per serving.

A super-fast, nutritious chilli with Quorn to up the
protein content. You could top it with Cheddar and
live Greek yoghurt, but don't forget to add the calories
(see page 239).

1. Heat the oil in a large non-stick frying or sauté
pan, add the onion and fry over a low-medium heat
for about 5 minutes, or until softened and lightly
browned, stirring regularly.

2. Add the mince, smoked paprika and cumin and cook
for a few seconds more, stirring.

3. Tip in the tomatoes, refill the empty can with water
and add this to the pan, too. Stir in the beans, crumbled
stock cube, tomato purée and herbs. Season well and
bring to a gentle simmer. Cook for 8–10 minutes, or
until the sauce has reduced and thickened, stirring
regularly, especially towards the end of the cooking time.

4. Adjust the seasoning to taste, scatter the coriander
leaves over the top, if using, and serve with lime wedges,
a large green salad and cauli-rice (see page 208).

Easy harissa chickpeas

SERVES **3** | **PREP** **5** mins | **COOK** **15** mins

2 tbsp olive oil
1 medium onion, peeled
   and finely chopped
2 tbsp harissa paste,
   ideally rose harissa
1 × 400g can chickpeas, drained
1 × 400g can chopped tomatoes
100g full-fat live Greek
   yoghurt

COOK'S TIP

You could serve this dish
with pan-fried halloumi,
if you like. Half a 250g
pack will be enough for
two (207cals per serving)
or top with some toasted
flaked almonds for an extra
77cals and 1.8g protein
for each tablespoon.

Tasty, immunity-boosting food straight from the
store cupboard. Harissa paste, with its sweet and
spicy, North African flavours, produces a richly
flavoured stew.

1. Heat the oil in a medium non-stick frying pan,
add the onion and gently fry over a low heat for about
5 minutes, or until well softened and beginning to
brown, stirring regularly.

2. Add the harissa paste and cook for a few seconds
more, stirring constantly. Stir in the chickpeas and the
tomatoes. Half fill the tomato can with water and add
to the pan. Season with salt and ground black pepper,
increase to a medium heat and bring to a simmer.
Cook for 10 minutes, or until the sauce reduces
and thickens, stirring regularly.

3. Serve with half a plate of freshly cooked finely sliced
green veg, or a salad, and the yoghurt spooned on top.

Veggie cottage pie

SERVES
4

PREP
15
mins

COOK
40
mins

1 tbsp olive oil
1 medium onion, peeled
   and finely chopped
200g carrots, well washed,
   trimmed and cut into
   1cm chunks
350g Quorn mince
1 vegetable stock cube
2 tbsp tomato purée
1 tsp dried mixed herbs
2 tsp cornflour
150g frozen peas
225g celeriac, peeled and
   coarsely grated (around
   175g prepared weight)
20g Parmesan, finely grated

COOK'S TIP

If you don't want to use
Quorn, try 2 × 400g cans
lentils instead. Or make the
pie with minced chicken or
turkey. Without the Quorn,
the recipe contains 147cals
and 6g protein per serving.

This comforting cottage pie is made with Quorn mince, but you could use canned or cooked lentils instead (see tip below). The grated celeriac makes an easy alternative to mash and can be used on top of any pie filling.

1. Heat the oil in a large, deep non-stick frying pan, add the onion and carrots and fry over a low-medium heat for 5 minutes, or until the onion is softened, stirring regularly.

2. Add the mince, crumble the stock cube over the top and stir in 650ml water. Add the tomato purée, herbs, a little salt and lots of ground black pepper. Bring to a simmer and cook for 10 minutes, stirring occasionally.

3. Meanwhile, preheat the oven to 220°C/fan 200°C/Gas 7.

4. Mix the cornflour with 1 tablespoon cold water in a small bowl. Add to the mince with the peas and cook for about 2 minutes, stirring, until the sauce is slightly thickened and glossy. Spoon into a 1.5-litre shallow ovenproof dish.

5. Place the grated celeriac and Parmesan in a large bowl and season with a pinch of salt and lots of ground black pepper. Mix well. Scatter on top of the mince and bake for about 20 minutes, or until the celeriac is tipped with brown and the filling is bubbling.

6. Serve with lots of green vegetables.

Simple Vegetable Sides

We would all benefit from eating more veg, particularly non-starchy veg, which do not cause a blood sugar spike. The idea of this chapter is to offer maximum flexibility, with recipes that can either be eaten as a side dish or provide a base for you to build a more substantial meal by adding protein (see page 239) and some complex carbs.

Simple dahl

SERVES **4** | PREP **5** mins | COOK **25** mins

4 tbsp canola oil
1 large or 2 small onions
   (around 200g), peeled
   and thinly sliced
20g fresh root ginger,
   peeled and finely chopped,
   or 1 tsp ground ginger
2–3 tsp medium curry powder
150g dried split red lentils
juice 1 small lemon (optional)

COOK'S TIP

To skip frying the onions
for the topping, cook the
full amount of onion in
2 tablespoons olive oil
until soft before adding the
ginger and curry powder.
The dahl will contain
205cals per serving.

Fast-cooking dried red lentils are invaluable to keep
at hand for thickening stews, adding to soups and,
of course, for making dahl. They add a bit of texture
and plenty of gut-friendly fibre. You can throw in extra
non-starchy veg to the dahl, such as spinach, mushrooms,
eggplant or cauliflower, or have them on the side,
without counting the extra cals. To transform it into
a main meal, serve it with one of the protein-rich
additions on page 239.

1. Pour the oil into a large saucepan and place over a high
heat. Add half the sliced onion and fry for 2–3 minutes, or
until lightly browned and crisp in places, stirring regularly.
Remove with a slotted spoon and set aside on a plate lined
with kitchen paper.

2. Reduce the heat, add the remaining onion, ginger
and curry powder and fry gently for 1 minute, stirring.

3. Add the lentils and 750ml cold water. Bring to a simmer,
then cover the pan, reduce the heat and cook for 15–20
minutes, or until the lentils are very soft, stirring regularly.

4. Season with salt and ground black pepper, drizzle with
lemon juice, if using, and scatter the crispy onions on top
to serve. Add a tablespoon of full-fat live Greek yoghurt
for 20cals.

Mediterranean-style broccoli

SERVES | **PREP** | **COOK**
3 | **5** mins | **4** mins

1 large head broccoli
(around 450g)
1 tbsp olive or canola oil
1 garlic clove, peeled and
thinly sliced
½–1 tsp crushed dried
chilli flakes
½ small lemon (around
2 tsp fresh lemon juice)
20g Parmesan, finely grated

This has to be the most popular vegetable side dish in our family. Crunchy, garlicky broccoli with some salty Parmesan and a hint of chilli. Perfect. It also makes a lovely light meal for two if you add protein (see page 239). This is delicious served cold as part of a salad the following day.

1. Third fill a large saucepan with water and bring to the boil.

2. Prepare the broccoli by cutting off all florets and slicing any large florets in half or quarters, until they are all roughly the same size. Discard the last 2.5cm of the stalk, then thinly slice the rest into pieces around 5mm thick. Add the broccoli to the pan and return to the boil. Cook for 1 minute. Drain well in a colander.

3. Place the oil in a large frying pan or wok over a medium-high heat. When the oil is hot, stir-fry the broccoli for 2 minutes, then add the garlic and chilli and cook for 1 minute more, stirring constantly.

4. Tip into a warmed bowl, season with a squeeze of lemon and lots of ground black pepper. Sprinkle with the Parmesan to serve.

Soy and sesame stir-fried veg

SERVES **2** | **PREP** **5** mins | **COOK** **5** mins

2 tsp olive or canola oil
75g green beans, trimmed
50g long-stemmed broccoli
    (around 3–4 spears), halved
    or quartered lengthways,
    depending on thickness
50g asparagus, trimmed
1 tbsp sesame seeds
    (around 10g)
1 tsp dark soy sauce
1 tsp sesame oil
lemon or lime wedges,
    to serve (optional)

A light and crunchy accompaniment to cooked meats and fish. It can be eaten cold as a salad and also works well as part of a packed lunch – just add protein (see page 239).

1. Heat the oil in a large frying pan or wok. Add the beans, broccoli and asparagus, and fry over a medium-high heat for 3–4 minutes, or until tender-crisp and lightly toasted in places. Stir and toss together regularly as they cook.

2. Sprinkle over the sesame seeds and fry for 1 minute more.

3. Remove from the heat, add the soy sauce and sesame oil, and toss together for a few seconds before serving with a squeeze of lemon or lime, if using.

COOK'S TIP

Some supermarkets sell selections of ready-prepared veg, so feel free to use one of these instead. Or use your own combination of green vegetables – just make sure the pieces are roughly the same size so they cook in the same time.

PER SERVING | **153cals** | PROTEIN **3.5g** | CARBS **12g** | FAT **9g** | FIBRE **5g**

Simple roasted veg

SERVES **4**

PREP **10** mins

COOK **30** mins

3 capsicums, any colour,
    deseeded and cut into
    2cm chunks
2 medium zucchinis,
    cut into 2cm chunks
2 medium red onions,
    peeled and each cut
    into 8 thin wedges
2 tbsp extra-virgin olive oil,
    plus extra for drizzling
    (optional)
1 tbsp fresh thyme leaves,
    from 2–3 sprigs thyme,
    or 1 tsp dried thyme

Luscious, multi-coloured Mediterranean veg.
Fabulous warm or cold, as a side dish or with extra
protein as a more substantial meal (see page 239).
This also makes an excellent base for a packed lunch.

1. Preheat the oven to 200°C/fan 180°C/Gas 6.

2. Place all the vegetables in a large bowl and toss with
the oil. Season with a large pinch of salt and lots of ground
black pepper. Scatter over a large baking tray in a single
layer and roast for 25 minutes.

3. Remove from the oven, scatter with the thyme and
turn all the vegetables. Return to the oven for a further
5 minutes, or until lightly browned.

4. Remove from the oven and drizzle with a little
extra-virgin olive oil just before serving, if you like
(adding the extra cals for each teaspoon).

PER SERVING | **174cals** | PROTEIN **11g** | CARBS **5g** | FAT **11g** | FIBRE **7g**

Brussels sprouts with bacon

SERVES **2** | PREP **5** mins | COOK **10** mins

2 tsp olive or canola oil
2 rashers smoked back bacon
   (around 75g), cut into
   1–2cm pieces
250g small Brussels sprouts,
   trimmed and halved
2 tsp cider vinegar

COOK'S TIP

Try sprinkling with Parmesan, or dotting with small chunks of soft blue cheese at the end for added protein, but add the extra calories (see page 239).

This much-maligned vegetable needs to be given another chance. The recipe here has converted most of our family, with Michael still on the fence. When fried quickly and retaining a bit of crunch, Brussels sprouts have a wonderful, delicate flavour.

1. Heat 1 teaspoon of the oil in a large non-stick frying pan, add the bacon and fry over a medium heat for 2–3 minutes, or until lightly browned, stirring regularly. Transfer to a plate with a slotted spoon.

2. Add the remaining oil and Brussels sprouts to the pan, reduce the heat slightly and fry gently for 4–6 minutes, or until browned in places and just tender, stirring often.

3. Return the bacon to the pan, sprinkle with the vinegar, add a pinch of salt and lots of ground black pepper and toss together for 1 minute before serving.

PER SERVING | **77cals** | PROTEIN **2g** | CARBS **7.5g** | FAT **3g** | FIBRE **5g**

Roasted vegetable wedges

SERVES
4

PREP
10
mins

COOK
30
mins

200g celeriac, well scrubbed
200g carrots, well washed
   and trimmed
200g beetroot, well scrubbed
   and trimmed
1 tbsp olive or canola oil

COOK'S TIP

Celeriac keeps well –
wrap the cut side and
keep in the fridge.

Missing your chips? Try this colourful selection
of lower-carb root veg instead. Don't bother peeling
them – you'll benefit from the extra nutrients and
fibre in the skin.

1. Preheat the oven to 220°C/fan 200°C/Gas 7.

2. Cut all the vegetables into wedges, roughly 1.5–2cm
wide and around 5–6cm long. They need to be similar
sizes so they cook at roughly the same rate.

3. Place in a bowl, add the oil, a couple of pinches salt
and lots of ground black pepper. Toss well together. Scatter
the veg over a large baking tray and roast for 20 minutes.

4. Remove from the oven, turn the wedges and roast for
a further 10 minutes, or until tender and lightly browned.

5. Serve with a high-protein, low-carb dish, or with
simply grilled or roasted meat or fish.

Creamy beans

SERVES | PREP | COOK
4 | **5** mins | **5** mins

2 × 400g cans organic
   butter beans in water
4 tbsp full-fat crème fraîche
1 tbsp finely snipped fresh
   chives (optional)

COOK'S TIP

If you are cooking for two,
simply half the ingredients.

These make a wonderful alternative to mash.
Serve them with any grilled or roasted meat
or fish; they are great with casseroles, too.

1. Place the beans and their water in a saucepan
and cook over a low heat for 3–4 minutes or until
hot, stirring regularly.

2. Drain in a colander then return to the pan and
add the crème fraîche and chives. Season with salt
and plenty of ground black pepper and toss together
over the heat for 20–30 seconds, or until hot, stirring.

3. Remove from the heat and either leave whole or
mash thoroughly with a potato masher, adding a splash
of hot water, if needed. You can also blitz with a stick
blender to achieve a smoother mash.

PER SERVING | **73cals** | PROTEIN **1.5g** | CARBS **12g** | FAT **0.5g** | FIBRE **6.5g**

Swede and carrot mash

SERVES | PREP | COOK
4 | **10** mins | **25** mins

550g swede, peeled and
cut into 3cm chunks
4 medium carrots
(around 300g), well
washed, trimmed, peeled
and cut into 2cm slices

COOK'S TIP

For a bit of a kick you
could stir in ½–1 teaspoon
crushed dried chilli flakes
to serve.

A versatile and creamy, orange-coloured mash, with
plenty of fibre. On a non-fast day, you could mash the
vegetables with a little butter or full-fat crème fraîche.

1. Place the swede and carrots in a large saucepan and
cover with cold water. Cover with a lid and bring to the
boil. Reduce the heat slightly and cook the vegetables for
20–25 minutes, or until softened, stirring occasionally.

2. Remove the pan from the heat and scoop out and
reserve a ladleful of water (roughly 6 tablespoons).
Drain and return the veg to the pan.

3. Add 4 tablespoons of the reserved cooking water
and blitz the veg to a smooth purée using a stick blender,
or cool slightly and blitz in a food processor, adding
a little extra water, if needed. You can also mash the
vegetables vigorously with a potato masher.

4. Season to taste with salt and ground black pepper.

Green rocket and celeriac mash

SERVES **2** | PREP **15** mins | COOK **20** mins

625g celeriac (around ½ large), well scrubbed and cut into 3cm chunks
1 garlic clove, peeled and halved
60g fresh rocket, watercress or baby spinach leaves
2 tbsp full-fat crème fraîche or full-fat live Greek yoghurt

COOK'S TIP

You can also mash vigorously with a potato masher, to produce a green-flecked appearance.

A vibrant, green accompaniment, which works well served with grilled or baked fish, chicken or meat. Enough for two generous portions or save some for the next day.

1. Third fill a saucepan with water and add the celeriac and garlic. Bring to the boil and cook for around 15 minutes, or until soft.

2. Add the leaves to the pan and allow to soften in the water for 20–30 seconds, then remove from the heat and drain very well in a colander. Leave to stand for 2–3 minutes.

3. Either return the vegetables to the pan and blitz with a stick blender, or tip into a food processor and blitz until almost smooth. Add the crème fraîche or yoghurt, a little salt and lots of ground black pepper and blitz again until smooth and creamy.

easy ways
with cauliflower

Highly nutritious and surprisingly rich in vitamin C and fibre, cauliflower has become a popular substitute for many starchy foods, such as rice and potato. Here we suggest three great ways to cook it – as cauli-rice, mash and roasted. For a couple of recipes on how to turn cauli-rice into a dish in its own right, see page 88. Or serve it with some added protein of your choice (see page 239).

Cauli-rice

PER SERVING | **68cals** | PROTEIN **5g**

SERVES 1
½ small cauliflower (around 200g)

1. Hold the cauliflower at the stalk end and coarsely grate in short, sharp movements in a downward direction. You can also do this in a food processor but don't let the pieces get too small or they will turn to a paste.

2. Either **stir-fry** with 1 teaspoon olive oil (27cals) in a large non-stick frying pan or wok over medium-high setting for 4–5 minutes, or **steam** in a saucepan over a medium-high heat for 3–4 minutes. You could also microwave on HIGH for 2–3 minutes. The rice should retain a bit of bite, like al-dente pasta.

3. Stir in some chopped parsley or coriander, or squeeze over some fresh lemon juice for added flavour.

Cauliflower mash

PER SERVING | **95cals** | PROTEIN **5g**

SERVES 1
½ small cauliflower (around 200g),
   trimmed, broken into small florets
   and stalk thinly sliced
1 tsp olive oil

1. Half fill a medium pan with water and bring to the boil. Add the cauliflower and return to the boil. Cook for 15–20 minutes or until very soft.

2. Drain, then return to the pan. Add the oil, a pinch of salt and lots of ground black pepper. Blitz with a stick blender, or cool slightly and blend in a food processor until smooth. (You can also mash vigorously with a potato masher.)

Roasted cauliflower

PER SERVING | **95cals** | **PROTEIN 5g**

SERVES 1

½ small cauliflower (around 200g),
  trimmed and broken into small florets,
  halving or quartering any large ones
1 tsp ground turmeric, or spices of your choice
1 tsp fresh lemon juice
1 tsp olive or canola oil

1. Preheat the oven to 220°C/fan 200°C/Gas 7.

2. Place the cauliflower, turmeric or other
spices and the lemon juice in a large bowl.
Drizzle with the oil and season with salt
and lots of freshly ground black pepper.
Toss together well, massaging the spice
into the florets.

3. Scatter the cauliflower over a large
baking tray and roast for 10–15 minutes,
or until just tender and browning in places.

PER SERVING | **258cals** | PROTEIN **7.5g** | CARBS **16.5g** | FAT **17.5g** | FIBRE **3g**

Hoisin roasted cauliflower with peanuts

SERVES	PREP	COOK
2	**10** mins	**15** mins

½ head cauliflower, trimmed and cut into small florets (around 300g prepared weight)
1 tbsp olive or canola oil
1 tbsp hoisin or plum sauce
½–1 tsp crushed dried chilli flakes
1 tsp finely grated fresh ginger or ½ tsp ground ginger
1 tbsp cider vinegar
25g plain peanuts, finely chopped
handful roughly chopped coriander leaves

A tasty Asian-inspired side dish, which works well with some added protein for a light lunch (see page 239). For extra flavour, serve with a portion of sauerkraut (see page 217) or kimchi – no need to count the calories.

1. Preheat the oven to 200°C/fan 180°C/Gas 6.

2. Scatter the cauliflower florets on a large baking tray and season well with a generous pinch of salt and lots of ground black pepper. Roast for 10 minutes, until starting to brown.

3. Meanwhile, place the oil, hoisin or plum sauce, chilli flakes, ginger and cider vinegar in a large bowl and mix well.

4. Remove the tray from oven and carefully transfer the hot cauliflower to the bowl to coat in the dressing. Return to the baking tray and scatter with the peanuts. Place back in the oven for another 5 minutes, until the cauliflower is starting to soften but still has a firm texture.

5. Scatter with the coriander to serve.

COOK'S TIP

Test for tenderness by inserting the tip of a knife into one of the thicker parts – it should slide in with only a little resistance.

Baked cabbage

SERVES
2

PREP
5
mins

COOK
15
mins

1 tbsp olive oil, plus extra
   for greasing
½ medium Savoy cabbage
   (around 350g)
lemon juice or soy sauce,
   to serve (optional)

Roasted cabbage tastes quite different to steamed. It has a sweet and slightly nutty, caramelised flavour. This makes a very simple main meal accompaniment, or you could scatter diced pancetta over the cabbage for the last 10 minutes of the cooking time and top with grated Parmesan just before serving – don't forget to add the extra calories.

1. Preheat the oven to 200°C/fan 180°C/Gas 6 and lightly grease a baking tray.

2. Cut the cabbage in half to make two large wedges, then place on the baking tray, cut side up. Drizzle with the oil, season with a little salt and lots of ground black pepper and bake for 15–20 minutes, or until just tender and browned in places.

3. Remove from the oven, sprinkle over a little lemon juice or soy sauce, if using, and serve straight away.

PER SERVING | **93cals** | PROTEIN **2g** | CARBS **6g** | FAT **6g** | FIBRE **4g**

Fennel and pak choi with ginger

SERVES	PREP	COOK
2	**10** mins	**15** mins

1 tbsp olive oil

½ medium onion,
   peeled and thinly sliced

½ medium fennel bulb,
   trimmed and thinly sliced

2 medium pak choi, trimmed
   and leaves separated

15g fresh root ginger
   (about 2cm), peeled
   and finely chopped

lemon wedges, to serve
   (optional)

COOK'S TIP

You can use a teaspoon of puréed ginger from a jar instead of fresh, if you like – simply add for the last minute of the cooking time.

A lovely side dish that makes a tasty accompaniment to plainly grilled meats and fish. The pak choi and fennel will boost your soluble and insoluble fibre intake and feed all those healthy microbes in your gut. For a more substantial meal, add toasted seeds, nuts or other protein (see page 208).

1. Heat the oil in a large non-stick frying pan, add the onion and fennel and fry over a low-medium heat for about 8 minutes, or until the fennel is beginning to soften, stirring occasionally.

2. Add the pak choi and ginger to the pan and cook for 5 minutes, or until the stalks are just softened but still have some crunch, turning regularly.

3. Season with salt and ground black pepper and add a squeeze of lemon juice, if you like, to serve.

Carrot, orange and cumin salad

SERVES **2** | PREP **10** mins

1 medium orange
2 medium carrots,
    well washed, trimmed
    and finely grated
½ small red onion, peeled
    and very finely sliced
2 generous pinches
    cumin seeds
1–2 pinches crushed
    dried chilli flakes
1 tsp cider vinegar
1 tbsp extra-virgin olive oil
small handful fresh mint
    leaves, chopped

This super-healthy, 1970s-inspired salad is fresh, zesty, juicy and bursting with vitamin C. You could up the protein content by adding diced cooked chicken breast, flaked smoked mackerel or roughly chopped cashews, pistachio nuts or toasted seeds to the salad (see page 239 for calories).

1. Cut the peel and pith from the orange and discard, then cut the orange into thin slices and place in a large bowl.

2. Add the remaining ingredients except the mint to the bowl, season with a little salt and lots of freshly ground black pepper, then toss together well.

3. Sprinkle with the mint to serve.

COOK'S TIP

To peel the orange, place it on a board and cut off the top and bottom. Stand it on one of the cut sides and slice off all the peel and pith.

easy ways
with pickles & sauerkraut

Fermentation is an ancient technique for preserving foods, using the natural healthy bacteria in the food (and is best done with organic veg, if available). The process encourages yeast and bacteria to break down the carbohydrates (sugars) in the vegetables. Fermentation also achieves another wonderful benefit: it produces natural probiotics, live micro-organisms, which support our gut microbiome and boost our immune system. We now eat live fermented kimchi, sauerkraut and pickles on a daily basis and love the tangy, sweet and salty flavours. These non-starchy veg, eaten in fairly small quantities, don't need calorie counting.

Build a pickle

Pickles are cheap, quick and easy to make – they are ready to eat in just over a week but last for ages in the fridge.

MAKES 500G
1 tbsp sea salt
filtered water
1 × 500ml jar with tight-fitting lid

Add 500g veg	Add 2–4 tsp any spices:
beetroot	turmeric (ground or grated fresh)
cabbage	cumin seeds
carrots	coriander seeds
cauliflower	black peppercorns
zucchini	grated fresh root ginger
cucumber	chilli flakes
onion	mustard seeds

COOK'S TIPS

To keep the salty water topped up, make extra brine by dissolving 1 teaspoon salt in 200ml filtered water.

Keep an eye on your pickle or kraut and discard any vegetables that have blackened or turned mouldy.

1. Rinse the veg in filtered water. Depending on your choice, trim your carrots/cucumber /zucchini, discard the outer leaves of your cauliflower and cabbage, and peel your onions. Slice the veg into 1–1.5cm cubes or batons, as appropriate, and place in a bowl.

2. Scatter with the salt and use your hands to rub the salt in. Leave the veg to soak for 30–60 minutes.

3. Stir in your choice of spices, then transfer the veg and juices to the jar, packing it in tightly.

4. Top up with filtered water so the veg are submerged – keep levels at least 2cm from the top of the jar.

5. Close the lid firmly and keep the pickle at room temperature for 5–10 days. Release the gases daily (burp them), especially in the first few days. Make sure the veg remain submerged and top the jar up with salty water (see tip), if necessary.

6. Taste regularly and, when it tastes nicely sweet and sharp, store in the fridge and eat within 2–3 months.

Build a kraut

Sauerkraut – fermented cabbage – goes well with almost any savoury food. We often have it with an omelette or scrambled eggs. This recipe is for turmeric and ginger sauerkraut but feel free to experiment with other spices, such as cumin, caraway, peppercorns, fennel, toasted coriander or mustard seed.

MAKES 1 LITRE
½ **medium white cabbage, quartered lengthways, hard core removed, finely sliced (or 1 small green pointed green cabbage, about 600g)**
2 **large white onions, peeled, halved and sliced**
1 **heaped tbsp sea salt**
2 **tsp grated fresh ginger**
1 **tsp ground turmeric**
2 × 500ml or 1 × 1 litre **clean jam jars with tight-fitting lids**

1. Combine the cabbage and onion in a large bowl, sprinkling the salt between the layers as you fill it. Massage the salt into the veg, then leave it for 1–2 hours to soften and release the liquor.

2. Stir in the ginger and turmeric. (This is the point to add other spices – see list opposite – if you want to flavour your kraut differently.)

3. Spoon the cabbage mixture and the juices into the jars. Pack the mixture down, pressing it firmly into the fluid – keep levels at least 2cm from the top of the jar. If there is not enough liquid to cover the mixture, top up with a few teaspoonfuls of filtered water. You can use a stone or piece of ceramic to keep the veg submerged.

4. Close the lid firmly, place the jars on a plate to catch any overflow and keep at room temperature, out of direct sunlight for 5–10 days. Release the gases daily (burp them), especially in the first few days. Make sure the veg remains submerged and top the jar up with salty water (see tip opposite), if necessary.

5. Sample regularly and, when it tastes good and tangy (usually 7–10 days), store in the fridge and eat within 2–3 months. Fermenting is a live process and occurs at different rates, according to the environment and temperature. Keep an eye on your kraut and discard any vegetables that have blackened or turned mouldy.

Occasional Treats

Cookies, desserts and chocolate tart? Yes – only ours are sweetened with whole fruit, so you get all the benefit of extra fibre and vitamins without the sugar spike. Enjoy them, in moderation, at the end of a meal. Remember, these are treats not snacks!

Ginger cookies

SERVES	PREP	COOK
14	**10** mins	**25** mins

2 medium egg whites
50g ground almonds
50g porridge oats
    (not jumbo oats)
50g coconut oil (or butter)
2 balls stem ginger in syrup,
    drained and finely chopped
2 tbsp stem ginger syrup
    from the jar

COOK'S TIP

If you have a mini food processor, you can halve the quantity to make 7 cookies instead.

Crunchy on the outside, soft and chewy on the inside, these delicious mini biscuits are surprisingly guilt free. They contain a decent hit of protein and fibre, are lovely as an after-dinner treat, or you can enjoy them crumbled in yoghurt with a handful of berries.

1. Preheat the oven to 180°C/fan 160°C/Gas 4 and line a large baking tray with non-stick baking paper.

2. Combine all the ingredients in a large bowl and mix together using a stick blender. You could also tip them into a food processor and blitz briefly to combine. The dough should be fairly soft. Alternatively, mix together by hand.

3. Use two dessertspoons to scoop out a little mixture and drop on to the lined tray. Press down into roughly 4cm rounds with the back of the spoon. Make a further 13 cookies in the same way. Bake for about 22–25 minutes, or until golden brown.

4. Cool for a few minutes before serving. Store excess cookies in an airtight container in the freezer.

No-added-sugar coconut and choc-chip cookies

SERVES	PREP	COOK
20	**15** mins	**15** mins

½ tsp canola or melted
   coconut oil
120g ground almonds
30g desiccated coconut
   (unsweetened)
60g coconut oil
1 large egg
½ tsp baking powder
½ tsp vanilla extract
40g soft pitted dates,
   finely chopped
40g dark choc chips
   (at least 70% cocoa solids)

COOK'S TIP

If you don't have dark
chocolate chips, use any
dark chocolate – as long
as it contains over 70%
cocoa solids – chopped
into small pieces.

Light and chewy, these coconut-flavoured biscuits
have a satisfying burst of chocolate. (See previous
page for photo.) A not-so-guilty treat!

1. Preheat the oven to 180°C/fan 160°C/Gas 4 and grease
a large baking tray with the canola or melted coconut oil.

2. Place all the ingredients, except the chocolate, in a
medium bowl, add a generous pinch of salt and blitz briefly
with a stick blender or in a food processor to make a slightly
sticky mixture. You may need to add ½ tablespoon water,
if the mixture is a bit crumbly. Alternatively, mix together
by hand.

3. Stir in the chocolate until well combined.

4. Roll the mixture into 20 small balls and place on the
greased tray. Flatten each of them until around 1cm thick,
then bake for about 15 minutes, or until firm and turning
deep golden brown around the edges.

5. Leave to cool on the tray for a few minutes, then transfer
to a wire rack. Store excess cookies in an airtight container
in the freezer.

Almond pancakes

SERVES | **PREP** | **COOK**
6 | **10** mins | **5** mins

25g wholemeal
    self-raising flour
50g ground almonds
½ tsp baking powder
1 medium egg
50ml full-fat milk
1 tsp canola oil, for frying

COOK'S TIP

The pancakes will keep
well in the fridge for
2 days and can be frozen.
Reheat in a dry frying pan
for 2–3 minutes, flipping
every now and then.
Or reheat on a plate
in the microwave.

**This is a protein-rich version of a traditional pancake.
They freeze brilliantly– so make a batch and just have
one as a treat.**

1. Place the flour, almonds and baking powder in a bowl,
stir well and make a well in the centre.

2. Crack in the egg and pour in half of the milk. Whisk very
well with a metal whisk. Add the remaining milk and whisk
again. Leave to stand for 5 minutes.

3. Brush a large non-stick frying pan with a little oil and
place over a medium-high heat. Pour a small amount of
the mixture in a heap on one side of the pan, then spread
it out with the back of a spoon; it should be around 7cm
in diameter. Make another 2 pancakes in the same way.
Cook for 1–1½ minutes, or until the tops start to look set
and bubbles begin to appear on the surface. Flip over and
cook on the other side for 1 minute, or until golden brown.

4. Transfer the pancakes to a small plate, cover with a
clean tea towel and keep warm while you make the rest.

5. Serve topped with mixed berries (19cals per 50g),
or Chia berry 'jam' (see page 237).

PER SERVING | **241cals** | PROTEIN **8g** | CARBS **9g** | FAT **19g** | FIBRE **2g**

Banana loaf

SERVES **12** | PREP **15** mins | COOK **50** mins

Many of us spent lockdown perfecting banana bread – including Justine. Here is a great one – nutty, delicious and surprisingly healthy.

2–3 very ripe bananas
(about 250g peeled weight),
mashed with a fork
2 large eggs, beaten
200g ground almonds
75g butter, melted,
or canola oil
50g wholemeal
self-raising flour
1 tsp ground mixed spice
1 tsp baking powder
75g mixed nuts or pecans,
roughly chopped (optional)

COOK'S TIP

You can freeze the extra slices to enjoy another time.

1. Preheat the oven to 180°C/fan 160°C/Gas 4 and grease and line the base and sides of a 900g/2lb loaf tin with non-stick baking paper.

2. Place the bananas in a large bowl and add the eggs, almonds, melted butter or oil, flour, spice and baking powder. Beat together well with a large metal whisk or electric beaters. Stir in the chopped nuts, if using. (You will need to add 17cals to each slice, if you do.)

3. Spoon the batter into the prepared tin and smooth the surface. Bake for about 50 minutes, or until a skewer inserted into the centre comes out clean.

4. Leave to cool in the tin for 10 minutes, then carefully turn out on to a wire rack. Serve in thin slices and store any excess in an airtight container in the freezer.

Chocolate and black bean torte

SERVES **12** | **PREP** **25** mins | **COOK** **25** mins

100g dark chocolate
    (at least 70% cocoa solids),
    broken into squares
100g coconut oil,
    plus extra for greasing
100g soft pitted dates
1 × 400g can black beans,
    drained and rinsed
3 large eggs, separated
¼ tsp cocoa powder,
    for dusting

COOK'S TIP

Keep in the fridge and
eat within a couple of
days, or freeze in slices.

Justine's deliciously light chocolate cake with an
ingredient that no one will guess. It's also gluten-free
and tastes luxurious without being too rich. Serve
in small wedges with a handful of raspberries.

1. Melt the chocolate in a heatproof bowl over a pan
of gently simmering water – make sure the bowl isn't
touching the water. (You can also melt the chocolate in
a microwave). Remove from the heat and leave to cool
for 20 minutes.

2. Preheat the oven to 190°C/fan 170°C/Gas 5 and grease
and line the base of a 20cm loose-based cake tin with
baking parchment.

3. Place the dates, oil and black beans in a food processor
and blitz until well combined. Add the egg yolks and blend
until as creamy and smooth as possible. You may need to
remove the lid and push the mixture down a couple of times.
Add the cooled, melted chocolate, followed by 100ml cold
water, in slow steady streams, until thoroughly combined.

4. Next, whisk the egg whites in a large clean bowl with
an electric whisk until stiff but not dry.

5. Stir a heaped tablespoon of the egg whites gently into
the chocolate mixture to soften, then transfer the chocolate
mixture to the bowl with the rest of the egg whites and
fold in gently using a large metal spoon, until thoroughly
combined. Spoon the mixture into the prepared cake tin
and spread to the sides. Bake in the centre of the oven
for 25 minutes, or until risen and firm to the touch.

6. Cool for 30 minutes, then remove from the tin. Sift over
the cocoa powder to dust and cut into small wedges to serve.

Crushed berry layer dessert

SERVES
4

PREP
10
mins

400g mixed berries, such
  as strawberries (hulled),
  blackberries, raspberries
  and blueberries
1 tbsp chia seeds
400g full-fat Greek yoghurt
1 tsp vanilla extract
2 tbsp flaked almonds,
  toasted (around 15g)

COOK'S TIP

If you are not eating these
straight away, cover and
keep in the fridge. Top
with the flaked almonds
just before serving. Eat
within a couple of days.

A gloriously creamy berry dessert scattered with
toasted almonds. Deceptively simple. Use a good-
quality full-fat live Greek yoghurt. On non-fast
days, you could use half crème fraîche and half
yoghurt, to make it even creamier.

1. Tip the berries into a bowl, keeping some back
for decoration. Mash lightly, then stir in the chia
seeds and leave to stand for 20 minutes.

2. Combine the yoghurt and vanilla extract in
a separate small bowl.

3. Layer the fruit and yoghurt into four glass
tumblers. Decorate with the reserved fruit
and top with flaked almonds.

PER SERVING | **225cals** | PROTEIN **4.5g** | CARBS **26g** | FAT **11g** | FIBRE **3g**

Spiced apple crisp

SERVES **4** | PREP **10** mins | COOK **5** mins

3–4 cooking apples, peeled, quartered, cored and cut into 2–3cm chunks (around 400g prepared weight)
60g sultanas
½ tsp ground cinnamon

For the topping
20g butter
40g flaked almonds
40g jumbo porridge oats

COOK'S TIP

This is delicious served with full-fat Greek yoghurt or full-fat crème fraîche (see page 239 for calories).

A comforting crumble-style dessert, which also tastes good served cold. It contains no added sugar – the sweetness comes from the sultanas. If you don't have sultanas, use raisins or chopped dates instead.

1. Place the apples, sultanas and cinnamon in a large saucepan. Add 100ml cold water, cover and cook over a medium heat for 5–6 minutes, or until the apples are soft but some chunks are just holding their shape, stirring occasionally.

2. Meanwhile, place the butter, almonds and oats in a non-stick frying pan and toast over a medium heat for 3–4 minutes, stirring regularly until lightly browned.

3. Divide the spiced apple between four dishes, sprinkle with the almond and oat mixture and serve.

Spicy nuts

SERVES	PREP	COOK
4	**5** mins	**10** mins

120g mixed nuts, such as Brazil nuts, cashews, hazelnuts and walnuts, any larger nuts roughly chopped
2 tsp canola or melted coconut oil
1 tsp medium curry powder
½ tsp crushed dried chilli flakes
½ tsp flaked sea salt

If you're not a fan of nuts, these will surely convert you. The trouble is they are very more-ish! You could scatter them on a salad or a curry for extra crunch and flavour. Nuts have substantial health benefits. Michael is a particular fan of Brazil nuts, as they are so high in the mineral selenium, which most of us are lacking. Selenium bolsters your immune system and thyroid function, as well as reducing inflammation and improving heart health.

1. Preheat the oven to 180°C/fan 160°C/Gas 4.

2. Place the nuts in a medium bowl. Add the remaining ingredients and lots of ground black pepper. Toss everything together until the nuts are lightly coated. Scatter over the baking tray and roast for 5 minutes.

3. Remove from the oven and turn the nuts. Roast for a further 5 minutes, or until the nuts are lightly browned. Take care they don't burn.

4. Cool for a few minutes on the tray to allow to crisp a little, then transfer to a bowl. Serve slightly warm or leave to cool completely.

Quick fruit salad

SERVES **6** | PREP **10** mins

1 × 400g can peach slices
   in natural juice
1 medium apple (around 150g),
   quartered, cored and
   finely sliced
2 clementines, satsumas
   or tangerines, peeled,
   halved from top to
   bottom and sliced
100g seedless grapes,
   any colour, halved

This may not be the most exciting fruit salad you
will ever make, but it's possibly the easiest. Serve
at the end of a meal to increase your daily intake
of fibre and vitamins, or add yoghurt and a handful
of nuts for an easy and filling breakfast, but don't
forget to add the calories (see page 239).

1. Place the peaches and their juice in a large bowl and
use the tip of a knife to cut each slice into 3–4 pieces.

2. Add the remaining ingredients, and toss together lightly.
Keep chilled until ready to serve.

PER SERVING | **102cals** | PROTEIN **3g** | CARBS **15g** | FAT **2.5g** | FIBRE **4g**

Baked nectarines with blackberries

SERVES **4** | **PREP** **5** mins | **COOK** **40** mins

4 ripe nectarines or peaches, halved and stoned

150g fresh or frozen blackberries

2 tbsp flaked almonds (around 15g)

COOK'S TIP

If you don't have blackberries, use raspberries instead.

This is one of our favourite summer desserts. It's incredibly easy to make and can be served warm or cold. It also makes a lovely, fruity breakfast, served with yoghurt and a sprinkling of sugar-free granola.

1. Preheat the oven to 200°C/fan 180°C/Gas 6.

2. Place the nectarine or peach halves in a small, shallow ovenproof dish or tin, cut side up. Sprinkle over 6 tablespoons of cold water. Scatter over the blackberries and the flaked almonds. Cover the dish with foil and bake for 30 minutes.

3. Remove the foil and bake for a further 5–10 minutes, or until the almonds are lightly toasted and the nectarines are very soft.

4. Serve warm or cold with full-fat Greek yoghurt (20cals per tablespoon) or crème fraîche (57cals per tablespoon).

PER SERVING | **115cals** | PROTEIN **3.5g** | CARBS **19g** | FAT **2g** | FIBRE **3g**

Wholemeal mini flatbreads

SERVES 4 | **PREP 15 mins** | **COOK 5 mins**

115g wholemeal plain flour,
   plus extra for rolling
½ tsp flaked sea salt
2 tsp olive or canola oil
75ml lukewarm water

COOK'S TIP

Make sure you do
not overcook these
flatbreads, so they
remain soft and pliable.

Surprisingly easy to make, these wholemeal flatbreads will give you less of a sugar spike than the standard white and processed options. Eat in moderation on non-fast days to accompany curries and chillies, or use as wraps for your favourite sandwich fillings.

1. Place the flour and salt in a medium bowl, add the oil and rub it in with your fingertips. Stir in the water and knead for 1–2 minutes, or until the dough feels smooth and elastic.

2. Turn the dough on to a lightly floured surface, divide into four and roll into small balls. Sprinkle the work surface with a little more flour and roll each ball very thinly, using a floured rolling pin, until they are around 17cm in diameter. Turn the dough regularly and sprinkle with a little more flour if it begins to stick.

3. Place a frying pan over a high heat and, when hot, add one of the flatbreads. Cook for about 30 seconds, then turn and cook on the other side for 20 seconds. It should be lightly browned in small patches and look fairly dry, without being crisp. Press the flatbread with a spatula while cooking to encourage it to puff up a little and cook inside.

4. Transfer the flatbread to a small plate, cover with a clean tea towel and keep warm while you make the rest.

Chia berry 'jam'

SERVES
6

PREP
5
mins

COOK
12
mins

50g soft pitted dates,
   roughly chopped
250g mixed berries, such as
   strawberries, raspberries
   and blackberries (fresh
   or frozen)
1 tbsp chia seeds
1 × 300ml heatproof, clean,
   lidded container or jar

COOK'S TIP

To give a zingier taste,
add a squeeze of lemon.

Chia deserves its name as a superfood for its fibre, protein and nutrient content (including omega-3 and calcium), but also for its curious ability to absorb fluid, forming a clear gel without flavour. It adds a smooth texture and thickens juices to make an instant jam. For a quick pudding, stir the jam into full-fat live Greek yoghurt.

1. Put 150ml cold water into a non-stick saucepan and add the dates. Bring to a gentle simmer and cook for 4–5 minutes, stirring constantly and pressing the dates against the pan until they soften.

2. Hull the strawberries, if using, and cut any larger fruit in half or quarter. Add all the fruit to the pan, sprinkle over the chia seeds and bring back to a gentle simmer. Cook for 6–8 minutes, stirring regularly and crushing the berries against the pan so they break up.

3. The 'jam' is ready when the fruit is very soft and looks thickened and glossy. If the jam begins to stick, add a splash more water.

4. Spoon into the container or jar and leave to cool before covering with a lid. Store in the fridge for up to 3 days or freeze portions and thaw as you need it.

Your Fast 800 toolkit

Traffic lights quick food check

A guide to help you see at a glance which foods are to be encouraged, which eaten in moderation and which to avoid. This is a rough guide only, as people respond differently to different foods.

green

Foods you can eat freely – calories still to be counted on fasting days on all but the non-starchy veg

- Non-starchy vegetables, including salad, leafy greens, broccoli, zucchinis, onions and mushrooms
- Fish
- Nuts and seeds
- Tofu
- White meat
- Extra-virgin olive oil and canola oil
- Herbs and spices
- Tomatoes, capsicums, peas and eggplants
- Full-fat fermented dairy: cheese, yoghurt, fromage frais (these are borderline orange – enjoy in moderation)
- Lowish-sugar fruit – berries and hard fruits (e.g. apples and pears), citrus fruits – preferably at the end of a meal

orange

Foods you can eat in moderation or occasionally

- Full-fat dairy: milk, butter
- Coconut oil or coconut milk
- Diced bacon or chorizo for garnish or flavour
- Eggs
- Beans, lentils, quinoa (NB these are in the green category if you are vegetarian)
- Whole grains
- Wholegrain seeded or sourdough bread
- Wholemeal/seeded pitta or flatbread
- Wholemeal pasta
- Wholemeal/ stoneground flour
- Unprocessed, unsweetened cereals
- Red meat (up to two times a week)
- Moderately starchy root veg: swede, parsnip, sweetcorn
- Butternut pumpkin, pumpkin
- Sweet tropical fruits (e.g. mango and pineapple)

red

Foods to avoid if possible

- Most pastries, cakes, snacks and biscuits
- White pasta/bread/rice
- White flour
- Highly processed foods
- Low-fat dairy products
- Highly processed oils, especially anything with trans fats
- Pre-prepared convenience food with lots of unrecognisable ingredients!
- Sugars and sweets

Easy ways to add protein

New research points to the importance of eating adequate amounts of protein – ideally at least 50g a day. It's harder for vegetarians to achieve their daily protein requirement on 800cals, so they may need to increase their intake to over 900 or 1000cals. Using a high-protein shake can help you stick to 800cals (see thefast800.com for more info on meal replacement shakes).

These simple, calorie-counted solutions are particularly useful if you haven't got time to cook a full recipe or you just want to beef up a plate of non-starchy veg.

Meat
75g cooked chicken breast
     (115cals, 22.5g protein)
2 slices roast turkey breast, around 50g
     (76cals, 17g protein)
1 tbsp diced chorizo, around 10g
     (40cals, 2.5g protein)
1 tbsp chopped fried bacon, around 7g
     (24cals, 1.5g protein)
2 thin slices ham, around 40g
     (43cals, 7g protein)
2 slices roast beef, around 80g
     (140cals, 26g protein)
4 slices salami or cured chorizo,
     around 20g (88cals, 4g protein)
1 rasher cooked back bacon, around 20g
     (61cals, 5g protein)

Fish
75g frozen cooked prawns, defrosted
     (52cals, 11.5g protein)
45g tuna, canned in oil (72cals, 11.5g protein)
3 drained anchovies in oil (17cals, 2g protein)
1 smoked mackerel fillet, around 70g
     (211cals, 15g protein)
2 slices smoked salmon, around 50g
     in total (92cals, 11.5g protein)
100g roasted or poached salmon
     (239cals, 24.5g protein)

Dairy & egg
1 medium boiled egg (78cals, 7g protein)
1 tbsp grated cheese, around 10g
     (41cals, 2.5g protein)
30g Cheddar (124cals, 7.5g protein)
30g halloumi, sliced, lightly fried in 1 tsp
     olive oil for 4–5 mins (130cals, 6g protein)
40g Greek-style yoghurt (53cals, 2g protein)
50g feta (124cals, 7.5g protein)
20g Parmesan, grated (82cals, 7g protein)
50g soft blue cheese, such as Roquefort,
     (187cals, 10g protein)
50g soft cheese, such as Brie
     (171cals, 10g protein)

Vegetarian
Handful of nuts, around 10g total
     weight, e.g. walnuts, pecans, hazelnuts
     (71cals, 2g protein)
15g almonds (95cals, 4g protein)
2 tsp sesame seeds, around 10g
     (63cals, 2g protein)
2 tbsp mixed seeds, around 20g
     (122cals, 5.4g protein)
100g tofu (123cals, 12.5g protein)
80g cooked edamame beans
     (110cals, 9g protein)
100g cooked puy lentils (143cals, 11g protein)
40g mushrooms fried in 1 tsp olive oil
     (33cals, 1g protein)
2 tbsp hummus, around 50g
     (160cals, 3.5g protein)
100g canned beans (109cals, 7g protein)
100g cooked lentils (143cals, 11g protein)
100g cooked quinoa (185cals, 6g protein)

How to make your greens even tastier

Green and non-starchy vegetables are so healthy and such an important part of the Fast 800 that we encourage you to eat these freely, filling half of your plate at each meal. Steam, boil or microwave them, and then try some of the following ideas to make them taste even better. We list both 'no-calorie-counting' options, for when you are at your 800cals limit, and low-calorie options for when you've got some calories going spare.

Examples of non-starchy greens and veg: cabbage, spring greens, chard, kale, pak choi, cavolo nero and spinach; as well as green beans, snowpeas, sliced zucchini or broccoli. And salad leaves of all colours – the more colourful, the better the nutritional value (and they look so enticing too).

Ways to add flavour with insignificant calories:
- Sea salt and a generous amount of black pepper
- A pinch of crushed dried chilli flakes
- A pinch of crushed garlic
- ½ tbsp soy sauce
- A squeeze of lemon or lime, e.g. on cabbage, broccoli or cauliflower
- ½ tbsp cider vinegar or balsamic vinegar, e.g. on spinach or cavolo nero
- A pinch of herbs
- I like to scatter little black nigella seeds on steamed veg, salads and slaws

Low-calorie ways to add flavour:
- 1 tsp butter – good on any veg (25cals)
- 1 tsp extra-virgin olive oil – good on any veg (27cals)
- 1 tsp hoisin sauce, e.g. on wilted spinach or cabbage (12cals)
- 1 tsp sesame or nigella seeds, e.g. on green beans or cabbage (32cals)
- 1 tsp grated Parmesan scattered on top, e.g. steamed broccoli (8cals)
- Jazz up greens by frying the veg in ½ tbsp olive oil with ½ garlic clove (you could add 1 tsp soy sauce, if you like), e.g. cabbage, snowpeas, broccoli or chard (52cals)
- Drizzle dressing on a large green or mixed salad – see Easy ways on page 61

Enjoy healthy complex carbs

Ditch the empty white stuff – white bread, pasta, potatoes and rice – and embrace complex carbs instead, which contain important nutrients and are an excellent source of fibre.

Healthy wholegrains, beans and lentils

As these foods often take longer to cook, you can save yourself time by cooking larger quantities and freeze them in portions. Try crumbling in half a stock cube during cooking for added flavour. Beans and pulses are a particularly good source of protein for vegetarians and, like wholegrains, they are good for gut bacteria too. We have included some wholegrains in small quantities in some of our recipes. But if you have calories to spare you might add 1 or possibly 2 tablespoons to a dish. On a non-fasting day, you can add 2–3 heaped tablespoons to your meal without counting.

Here are a few options:
- 1 tbsp cooked brown rice (21cals)
- 1 tbsp cooked quinoa (18cals)
- 1 tbsp cooked bulgur wheat (13cals)
- 1 tbsp cooked puy lentils (18cals)
- 1 tbsp cooked pearl barley (19cals)

OTHER LOW-CARB SWAPS

- **Cauliflower** makes an excellent swap as it's very low in calories and high in nutrients. It's also remarkably flexible. We love it. See page 208 for three Easy ways with cauliflower.
- **Zoodle spaghetti** (100g) 20kcals Allow 1 zucchini per person. See pages 120 and 114 for ways to cook this.
- **Green rocket and celeriac mash** (see page 207)
- **Swede and carrot mash** (see page 206)
- **Celeriac chips** (see page 150)
- **Roasted vegetable wedges** (see page 204)
- **Creamy beans** (see page 205)
- **Cabbage linguine** Use ¼ Savoy cabbage for 2 people. Remove the core, finely slice the cabbage then steam for about 5 minutes or in the microwave for less. You want it to be al dente.
- **Konjak 'Zero' noodles or spaghetti** (Shiritaki). Originally from Japan, these contain remarkably few calories and plenty of fibre. They are available in most large supermarkets.

The *Fast 800 Easy* stores

As I said in my introduction, fresh meat and fruit and veg may be nice to have, but I'm also a big fan of cooking from stores. Frozen veg, such as peas, spinach or cauliflower florets, are already conveniently prepared and chopped; they provide high-quality nutrients and, because they last for many weeks in the freezer, you know they're always available. Likewise, tins of chickpeas, tomatoes, tuna or jars of red capsicums are brilliant staples, sitting there, ready to be pulled out of the cupboard and thrown together for a quick meal.

Remember, if you have the right foods to hand, you are much less likely to get side-tracked or tempted by unhealthy ones. This list is intended as a guide. Please don't feel you have to go out and buy every item on it! Be selective and start with the foods you think you are most likely to eat.

Oils & vinegars
Extra-virgin olive oil, or the least refined oil you can afford
Cold-pressed canola (for high temperature frying)
Coconut oil
Cider vinegar
Balsamic vinegar

Canned
Tomatoes
Chickpeas
Coconut milk
Beans: kidney, mixed beans, haricot, butter beans, black beans
Puy lentils
Fish: tuna, sardines, salmon, mackerel, anchovies

Dried
Stock cubes
Wholemeal flour
Baking powder
Wholegrains
Oats
Brown/red/black or wild rice
Pearl barley
Quinoa
Puy lentils, red lentils

Jars & bottles
Red capsicums
Piquant peppadew peppers
Capers
Jalapeños
Stem ginger in syrup

Herbs & spices
Oregano or mixed herbs
Thyme
Medium curry powder
Cumin seeds
Ground turmeric
Smoked paprika
Black pepper
Chilli flakes
Sea salt

Nuts & seeds
Mixed unsalted nuts
Ground almonds
Flaked almonds
Cashews
Walnuts
Pecans
Mixed seeds

Flavourings, sauces & pastes
Harissa paste
Pesto
Thai red or green curry paste
Medium curry paste
Dark soy sauce
Tomato purée
Plum sauce
Soy or tamari sauce
Hoisin sauce
Miso paste

Frozen
Chicken breasts
Prawns
Spinach
Peas
Edamame
Mixed veg
Raspberries, mixed berries
Broccoli, cauliflower

Fridge
Eggs
Full-fat live Greek yoghurt
Cheese – mature Cheddar, goat's cheese, feta, Parmesan, halloumi
Leafy greens and salad
Fresh garlic
Fresh ginger
Parsley
Coriander
Cooked chicken
Chorizo
Bacon
Smoked mackerel
Lemons and limes
Full-fat mayo
Mustard
Sauerkraut

Sweet things
Soft pitted dates
Maple syrup
Vanilla extract
Dark plain chocolate ideally 85%

Making meals work for the whole family

Because the Fast 800 programme is based on a healthy, lowish-carb Mediterranean-style diet, it is extremely flexible – whether you want to bump up a low-calorie recipe to eat on a non-fasting day or to feed other members of your household. While Michael was doing some 800-calorie days during lockdown, we all ate together, often using the recipes in this book as I was testing them – the children and I eating freely, while Michael skipped any starchy carbs, like bread or potatoes, and occasionally ate a couple of tablespoons of brown rice, quinoa or puy lentils.

The simple message is that you can expand the portion sizes of our recipes and add in extras where and how you wish.

When you are making a meal such as a stew, curry or a substantial salad, simply double up portions and/or add a veg side dish (see pages 196–214) and/or extra protein (see page 239). Breakfast may be doubled up, too, or become a brunch or lunch.

Soups are wonderfully adaptable – add toasted seeds, bacon, chorizo or grated cheese (see page 239 for more tasty and high-protein toppings) and/or a slice of wholemeal seeded bread.

Increase your complex carbs, such as beans, lentils and wholegrains, by adding an extra 2–3 heaped tablespoons of these foods on a non-fasting day and encourage the rest of the family to eat these, too.

When it comes to bread, it's about choosing carefully, as white bread and a slice of seeded wholemeal sourdough are two entirely different species, and this is as true for your non-dieting family, as it is for you. Encourage them to choose wholegrain, seeded or sourdough wherever possible.

Equally, urge all the family to choose fruit which is moderately low in sugar, like berries, apples and pears, and to enjoy these with live, full-fat Greek yoghurt.

7-DAY MEAL PLANS
2 or 3 meals a day, with or without meat

These meal plans are intended to give you a taste of how the different options might work. Do feel free to use up your leftovers and swap in different recipes you like the look of and to repeat days, so you don't have to cook two days in a row – whatever best suits you. Just keep an eye on the nutritional information on the recipe pages to make sure you are keeping protein high (more than 50g daily if you can) and starchy carbs and sugar lowish (try not to go over 75g carbs on most days and ideally keep it below 50g).

Remember, the 800cals a day is just a ballpark figure – aim for somewhere between 800 and 900 calories a day. Calories, although useful, are not an accurate science and there is considerable variation between calorie counters. So, going over by 40–50cals here and there is not going to make a significant difference to your rate of weight loss. Just remind yourself that any reduction below 1000cals a day is going to have a substantial impact. And beyond that, it's the quality of the food that really matters. Eating 800cals of pastries is going to be far worse for you than 1000cals on a Med-style diet.

You will see that in the meat-free plans the daily calorie totals tend to be higher, between 900 and 1000, which is fine. This is to ensure adequate daily protein is included. If you are vegetarian, you may wish to swap in a suitable high-protein shake to top up your protein (see thefast800.com for options); and if you are vegan, adding in high-protein shakes may be the only way to do this diet.

On days when you have calories to spare, you might want to choose a dressing for your salad or try some of the other ideas on page 240 to jazz up your non-starchy vegetables. You can also include a portion of hard fruit, such as an apple or pear, or a handful of berries, to take you just over the 800cals – eat this either with breakfast or straight after a meal. You will see that on some days in the 2- and 3-meal plans, the daily calorie quota falls far enough below the 800cals mark for you to have a treat (see pages 220–37).

The important thing, if you want to encourage fat-burning, is to stick to a lowish-carb diet, avoid snacking between meals, and ideally add in some Time Restricted Eating (see page 16 for more on this).

2 meals a day

DAY 1
	cals	protein
One Pan Breakfast p44	227	15.7g
Serve with a thin slice wholegrain toast	71	3.1g
Fastest Spaghetti Bolognese p144	426	57g
Serve with an extra tbsp Parmesan	62	5.8g
	786	**81.6g**

DAY 2
	cals	protein
Med Veg and Parmesan Omelette p172	382	24.5g
Lamb and Chickpea Curry p157	418	33g
	800	**57.5g**

DAY 3
	cals	protein
Warm Chicken and Avocado Salad p70	367	43g
Quick Fruit Salad p232	59	0.5g
Pesto Fish p105	391	29g
	817	**72.5g**

DAY 4
	cals	protein
Kipper with Poached Egg and Spinach p41	360	32g
Tex-Mex Chicken Bean Bowls p137	380	45.5g
Serve with a portion of cauli-rice p208	68	5g
	808	**82.5g**

DAY 5
	cals	protein
Avocado, Crispy Bacon and White Bean Salad p74	467	16g
Cardamom Chicken p141	305	31g
Serve with Wholemeal Flatbread p236	115	3.5g
	887	**50.5g**

DAY 6
	cals	protein
Tuna, Bean and Roasted Capsicum Salad p68	229	20g
Steak and Chips p150	358	41.5g
Crushed Berry Layer Dessert p229	212	8g
	799	**69.5g**

DAY 7
	cals	protein
Sweet Chilli Salmon with Edamame p102	436	34g
Creamy Chicken and Mushrooms p139	326	39g
Serve with Roasted Veg Wedges p204	77	2g
	839	**75g**

3 meals a day

DAY 1
	cals	protein
Nutty Seedy Porridge p28 (made with 100ml milk)	294	11.5g
Low-carb Portobello 'Pizzas' p78	287	15.5g
Roast Chicken with Mixed Greens p126	246	36g
	827	**63g**

DAY 2
	cals	protein
Scrambled Egg Stuffed Mushrooms p33	264	20g
Leek and Celeriac Soup p50	123	4g
Fastest Spaghetti Bolognese p144	426	57g
	813	**81g**

DAY 3
	cals	protein
Universal Green Shake p31 (made with 1 tbsp chia seeds)	186	4.4g
Tuna and Roasted Red Capsicums p84	193	19g
Pork with Mustard & Cider Vinegar p168	288	34g
Serve with Swede and Carrot Mash p206	73	1.5g
	740	**58.9g**

DAY 4
	cals	protein
Smoked Haddock Brunch Pots p39	249	22g
Prawn and Pasta Salad p69	360	21g
Quick Veggie Chilli p191	232	19g
	841	**62g**

DAY 5
	cals	protein
Sardines with Tomatoes on Sourdough p43	239	15.5g
Miso Soup with Prawns p54	69	12g
Individual Moussakas p161	437	27g
	745	**54.5g**

DAY 6
	cals	protein
Poached Eggs with Avocado & Bacon p40	250	12.5g
Prawn Zoodles with Chilli & Lemon p118	271	21.5g
Cardamom Chicken p141	305	31g
	826	**65g**

DAY 7
	cals	protein
Fruit 'n Nut Granola p26 (made with 75g yoghurt and 30g fruit)	287	8.5g
Low-carb Portobello 'Pizzas' p78	287	15.5g
Simple Beef Casserole p156	307	35g
	881	**59g**

2 meals a day Vegetarian

DAY 1	cals	protein
Jalapeno, Spinach and Parmesan Omelette p36	300	23g
Crunchy Rainbow Salad with Cashews and Ginger p62	495	13g
Serve with 50g halloumi fried in ½ tsp oil	186	10g
	981	**46g**

DAY 2	cals	protein
Lightly Curried Cauli-rice p88	323	25g
Halloumi Baked Zucchinis p173	392	22.5g
Top with 20g toasted almonds	132	5g
	847	**52.5g**

DAY 3	cals	protein
Lentil, Feta and Beetroot Salad p66	382	21g
Cheese and Spinach Mini Muffins x 3 p32	213	15g
Serve with Roasted Veg with Cumin and Goat's Cheese p177	340	16.5g
	935	**52.5g**

DAY 4	cals	protein
Tofu Mushroom Ramen p174	339	21.5g
Leek, Pea and Paneer Curry p181	410	21g
Serve with 30g Greek yoghurt	40	2.6g
and 20g toasted almonds	132	5g
	921	**50.1g**

DAY 5	cals	protein
Feta, Pea and Mint Crustless Quiche p82	340	17g
Serve with a slice of Banana Loaf p224	241	8g
Chinese-style Egg-fried Cauli-rice p88	362	28g
	943	**53g**

DAY 6	cals	protein
Easy Frittata p80	294	22.5g
Serve with Med-style Broccoli p197	188	13g
Tomato and Basil Salad with Whipped Goat's Cheese p64	442	17g
	924	**52.5g**

DAY 7	cals	protein
Med Veg and Parmesan Omelette p172	382	24.5g
Serve with a portion of Spicy Nuts p231	193	8g
One Pan Miso Eggplant & Peanuts p178	421	21.3g
	996	**53.8g**

3 meals a day Vegetarian

DAY 1	cals	protein
Cheese and Spinach Mini Muffins x 3 p32	213	15g
Low-carb Portobello 'Pizzas' p78	287	15.5g
Curried Broccoli with Paneer p182	345	21g
	845	**51.5g**

DAY 2	cals	protein
Nutty Seedy Porridge p28 (made with 100ml milk)	294	11.5g
Med Veg and Parmesan Omelette p172	382	24.5g
Veggie Cottage Pie p193	238	19g
	914	**55g**

DAY 3	cals	protein
Jalapeño, Spinach and Parmesan Omelette p36	300	23g
Spiced Chickpea, Tomato and Spinach Salad p59	314	14.5g
Mushroom & Chestnut Bourguignon p180	382	17g
	996	**54.5g**

DAY 4	cals	protein
Scrambled Egg Stuffed Mushrooms p33	264	20g
Lentil, Feta and Beetroot Salad p66	382	21g
Quick Veggie Chilli p191	232	19g
	878	**60g**

DAY 5	cals	protein
Boiled egg x 2 with asparagus p34	234	30g
Harissa Lentil and Chickpea Soup with Spinach p56	206	10g
Halloumi Baked Zucchinis p173	392	22.5g
	832	**62.5g**

DAY 6	cals	protein
Universal Green Shake p31 (made with 1 tbsp chopped mixed nuts)	115 60	2.5g 2.7g
Chinese-style Egg-fried Cauli-rice p88	362	28g
Leek, Pea and Paneer Curry p181	410	21g
	947	**54.2g**

DAY 7	cals	protein
Granola (made with 75g yoghurt) p26	276	8.5g
Easy Frittata p80	294	22.5g
One Pan Miso Eggplant & Peanuts p178	421	21.3g
	991	**52.3g**

Index of recipes by calories

Index

DR CLARE BAILEY, wife of Michael Mosley, is a GP who has supported hundreds of patients to lose weight, reduce their blood sugars and put their diabetes into remission at her surgery in Buckinghamshire. She is the author of the bestselling *8-Week Blood Sugar Diet Recipe Book*, *Clever Guts Diet Recipe Book* and *The Fast 800 Recipe Book*. Instagram @drclarebailey

JUSTINE PATTISON is one of the UK's leading healthy-eating recipe writers. She has published numerous books – she worked with Clare on *The Fast 800 Recipe Book* – makes regular appearances on television, can often be heard on the radio and contributes to many top magazines, newspapers and websites. www.justinepattison.com

OTHER BOOKS AVAILABLE IN THIS SERIES:

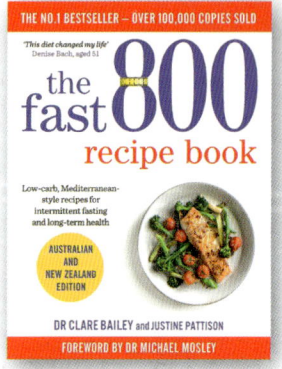